Mushy!
The Complete Book of Valentine Words

by Lynda Graham-Barber

Pictures by Betsy Lewin

BRADBURY PRESS
New York

Collier Macmillan Canada
Toronto

Maxwell Macmillan International Publishing Group
New York   Oxford   Singapore   Sydney

Bradbury Press
Macmillan Publishing Company
866 Third Avenue
New York, NY 10022

Collier Macmillan Canada, Inc.
1200 Eglinton Avenue East
Suite 200
Don Mills, Ontario M3C 3N1

Printed and bound in the United States of America
First Edition
10 9 8 7 6 5 4 3 2 1

Book design by Amy Hill

LIBRARY OF CONGRESS CATALOGING-IN-PUBLICATION DATA
Graham-Barber, Lynda.
Mushy! : the complete book of Valentine words / by Lynda Graham-
Barber ; pictures by Betsy Lewin. — 1st ed.
p.   cm.
Includes bibliographical references.
Summary: Defines or explains various words commonly associated
with Valentine's Day, such as "Cupid," "heart," and "romance," and
gives their origin or historical background.
ISBN 0-02-736941-2
1. Saint Valentine's Day—Juvenile literature. 2. English
language—Etymology—Juvenile literature. [1. Valentine's Day.
2. English language—Etymology.] I. Lewin, Betsy, ill. II. Title.
GT4925.G73   1991
394.2'683—dc20   90-33047 CIP AC

For Mom, Kis, and Ray, "Mr. Swoon"

If a book comes from the heart,
it will continue to reach other hearts.

—Thomas Carlyle

Contents

....

Saint Valentine's Day
is celebrated on the
fourteenth of
February.

Saint Valentine's Day

It's February 14. There's not a red rose or a chocolate-covered cherry left in town. Classroom walls are papered with red hearts, and judging by the stack of cards in the postal carrier's bag, it looks like Christmas all over again.

Happy Saint Valentine's Day—the day we celebrate love. But how did this popular holiday get wrapped up in lace and satin in the first place? The answer or answers, which span centuries, are surrounded by so many myths and legends that the real story may never be known.

At the heart of the debate are three possible explanations. To explore the first one, let's leave the decorated classrooms and depleted candy shops and travel to ancient Rome, back to the third century A.D.

It was a time when plague, famine, and war threatened to overthrow the vast and powerful Roman Empire. It was also the period when pagan Roman emperors sentenced Christians to death for practicing their religious beliefs. One of these emperors was Claudius II, who reigned for only a brief span, from A.D. 268–270. He was called Claudius the Goth because he successfully stopped the advance of the invading Goths from the north. However, for our story, at least, Claudius is

more important as the ruler who collided with a priest of unshakable determination. His name was Valentine.

In the Catholic church's official record books on saints, there are eight Saint Valentines in all. The two main claimants to the holiday throne are a Roman priest named Valentine and Valentine of Terni, a bishop. Both Valentines are said to have been martyred in Rome on the very same day. Little is known of Bishop Valentine, except that he suffered from epilepsy. In some parts of Germany today, epilepsy is still called Valentine's sickness.

This brings us to the Roman priest Valentine. According to a fanciful work composed in the fifth and six centuries, the priest Valentine stood his ground with Claudius and refused to abandon his religious views. As a result, the emperor had Valentine beaten, stoned, and, finally, beheaded. He died on February 14, A.D. 269.

But what does a martyred priest have to do with red roses and romance? As one romantic legend has it, the priest Valentine got into trouble for playing Cupid. In this account, Emperor Claudius canceled all scheduled marriages because he was having trouble raising soldiers for his army. The men, it seemed, did not want to leave their sweethearts to go out and defend Rome from its enemies. A sympathetic Valentine, so the story goes, defied the emperor's decree when he continued to marry couples secretly. When Claudius found out, he was furious and threw Valentine into prison.

In another, even more far-fetched tale, Valentine himself succumbed to Cupid's arrow when he fell in love with his jailer's blind daughter. Valentine reportedly cured her of her blindness and wrote love letters from prison signed, "From your Valentine."

These stories make for interesting reading, but they have been discounted by authorities. Historians believe that to understand the most likely link between the persecuted saint and the Valentine holiday, we must again return to Rome, to an ancient Roman pagan festival called Lupercalia.

Lupercalia, which was celebrated beginning February 15, may have honored Lupercus, the god of animals, forests, and shepherds. In one ceremony, priests called Luperci first sacrificed two goats, then cut strips from the goat skins. Festival priests considered these strips magical instruments of purification and would run through the streets touching or striking anyone they passed. Women were especially eager, believing that if they were touched by the magical strip, their fertility would be ensured.

In another festival ceremony, it's said someone dropped the names of young Roman maidens into an urn. Young men then reached down into the urn and drew a name. The name a young man picked was to be his partner for the festival, or perhaps longer if the two hit it off. Could this Roman urn have been the very first valentine box?

Lupus is Latin for "wolf" and is thought to be the basis of the word *Lupercalia*, which means "festivals of the wolf." According to another popular Roman story, a female wolf nursed the twins Romulus and Remus, legendary founders of Rome, in a cave. The Romans also believed wolves possessed strong sexual powers. A flirtatious man is sometimes called a wolf. And to catch a woman's attention, such a "wolf" might signal with, what else, a wolf whistle!

During the spread of Christianity in the fifth century A.D., some two hundred years after Valentine died, Pope Gelasius I was busily trying to convert pagan festivals into religious ones. In order to give the pagan festival of Lupercalia a more Christian slant, the pope is thought to have come up with the idea of substituting the names of saints for the names of young women. The saint drawn during Lupercalia was to serve as the young man's role model for the rest of the year. Some historians believe the pope then linked Valentine's name to the festival because February 14, the anniversary of his death, was coincidentally the day before Lupercalia began. So it became official in A.D. 494—pagan Lupercalia became the Christian feast of purification.

Can you imagine the disgusted looks on the faces of young Roman men who, expecting to draw Cornelia or Beatrice, got Saint Benedict instead? Richard LeGallienne, writing in 1892, agreed that ". . . to expect a woman and to draw a saint is ever a disappointment to mortal man."

The setting for the second explanation of the roots of Saint Valentine's Day is ancient and medieval Europe. According to popular legend, people at that time believed that the birds began claiming their mates on February 14. So, they drew the conclusion that if the birds were romantic on February 14 and priest Valentine died on that day, then Valentine and courtship, or romance, were forever linked. As the late fourteenth-century poet Geoffrey Chaucer (c. 1343–1400) wrote in his long poem *Parliament of Fowls:* "For this was Seynt Valentyne's day / When every foul [bird] cometh ther to choose his mate."

Some scholars dismiss this theory as strictly for the birds! After all, we know that birds begin to mate in the spring, not in the middle of winter. Just recently, one historian poked more holes in this theory. He believes it was Chaucer himself who linked Saint Valentine with bird courtship and love. But Chaucer's Saint Valentine was not the priest you just read about but yet another Valentine. (Remember, there were eight.) This Valentine died on May 3, a much warmer time when birds are singing exuberantly for their spouses. Have a heart! Will the real Saint Valentine please step forward?

Well, if you don't buy either of these two explanations,

you might like the third: the word mix-up theory. The Norman-French word *galatin* means "a lover of the fair sex." Since the letter *g* was often pronounced *v*, *galatin* evolved to be spoken and written as *valatin*, or *valentine*. So the conclusion—and a pretty shaky one at that—was that anyone with the name Valentine had ties to romance.

Maybe all three theories add up to one big mushy triangle!

The Valentine
How-Did-It-All-Begin Chart

THEORY ONE
....

Setting: ancient Rome
Event: Pope Gelasius I links pagan festival of Lupercalia to Saint
      Valentine's Day; the valentine box is filled with saints' names

THEORY TWO
....

Setting: ancient and medieval Europe
Event: association of unlikely bird courtship with February 14,
      anniversary of Saint Valentine's death

THEORY THREE
....

Setting: medieval France
Event: word *galatin*, "lover of fair sex," evolves to *valatin* then *valentine*

SOME DATES TO KEEP IN MIND AS YOU READ THIS BOOK

Old English Period (450–1100)

Language spoken by Germanic tribes that migrate to Britain in the fifth century. Earliest documents are from the seventh century. Old English prevails until roughly 1100, when it evolves into Middle English and incorporates large numbers of Latin and Norman-French words—the "borrowed" French language of the Scandinavian Norsemen living in Normandy who subjugated Britain during the Norman Conquest in 1066.

Middle English Period (1100–1500)

Parisian French and Latin continue to influence language during this period, roughly extending from the twelfth century through the fifteenth century.

Modern English Period (1500–Present)

This period begins at the start of the sixteenth century and extends to the present day. During this time spelling is standardized, thanks to the printing press, and vowel patterns change to those we recognize today. Latin and, increasingly, Classical Greek words and roots continue to be incorporated into the English language.

February

The word *February* comes from the Latin *februare*, "to cleanse." In the old Roman calendar, February was the last month of the year, and March was the first. In order to welcome the New Year, the Romans believed they should undergo a process of purification and cleansing, not only for themselves but for their land and livestock as well.

As we read earlier, one of these mid-February Roman purification festivals was called Lupercalia. During Lupercalia, the festival priests used their magical goatskin strips, called *februa*, or "purifiers," as instruments for cleansing and fertility. So February became the "month of purification."

Do You Know?

Julius Caesar's (100–44 B.C.) astronomers set the solar year at 365 days and six hours, thereby establishing the Julian calendar This meant that every four years, the six hours would accumulate to equal a twenty-four-hour day. This "extra" day was added to the shortest month, February, which is why there is a leap year every four years.

Anglo-Saxons called February *Sprote Kalemonath*, or "sprout kale-month," because it was the time when cabbages sprouted. Have you ever eaten kale? It's a cabbage with pretty curly leaves and a slightly bitter taste.

Down with *Cupid*
and that squawking
Turtledove;
you won't catch me
falling in *Love*!

Cupid

No Valentine's Day celebration would be complete without that plump little boy pulling back his bow to fire off a sling full of love arrows. In fact Cupid is almost as inseparable from February 14 as the saint himself!

The word *Cupid* comes to us from the Latin word *Cupido*, or *Cupid*. In Roman mythology, Cupid, the son of the goddess of love and beauty, Venus, is the god of romantic love; that is, love outside the sphere of the saints. Cupid is depicted on valentines, jewelry, and in paintings as a fat-cheeked little boy with wings, either blind or blindfolded. Armed with his bow, Cupid shoots invisible arrows into his victims, who then fall hopelessly—or blindly—in love.

In one of the most famous Roman myths starring Cupid, he appears as a young man rather than a troublesome boy. Every night he visits Psyche, who loves him desperately. He leaves each morning but says he will always return as long as she doesn't try to look at him. Overcome by curiosity one night, Psyche lights a lamp. A drop of hot oil falls onto the sleeping Cupid's shoulder and he flees. Psyche wanders for years looking for Cupid. In the end, the lovers are reunited.

Gods and Goddesses of Love

NAME	PLACE OF ORIGIN	CHARACTERISTICS
Cupid	Ancient Rome	son of Venus, mischievous, chubby-cheeked boy with a golden quiver full of arrows tipped with love potion
Kama	India	beautiful young man armed with a bow made of sugar cane and a bowstring of bees, each arrow tipped with a distinct flower; rides on a parrot; in Hindu, *kama* means love or desire
Ishtar	Ancient Babylonia	radiantly beautiful mother goddess of both sexual love and war; often shown with a lion and symbolized by an eight-pointed star; descended into the underworld searching for her love

....

Astarte (Ashtoreth)	Ancient Phoenicia	a love goddess with crescent horns, seated on a throne flanked by sphinxes; closely associated with Ishtar
Erzulie	Haiti	a powdered and perfumed love goddess or spirit with three wedding rings on her fingers, one for each husband; shown weeping over life's beauty and love's limitations
Yarilo (or Erilo)	Eastern Europe (Slavonic)	dressed in a white cloak, a young man riding on a white horse
Tlazolteotl	South America	Aztec love goddess also known as the dirt goddess because of her association with lust; her forehead is bound and she wears cotton earrings

Eros	Ancient Greece	a young man, often with golden wings and arrows; a mature version of Cupid; represents the unifying power of love
Freyja	Northern Germany (Norse)	wears a cloak and has falcon's wings, riding a cat-drawn chariot; deserted by her husband because she chose material wealth over his love
Venus	Ancient Rome	goddess of love and beauty, mother of Cupid; doves or swans draw her chariot
Aphrodite	Ancient Greece	goddess of love and marriage; according to some accounts, born of sea foam and depicted on a scallop shell; beloved of Adonis

Turtledove

Robin Finch and Jay Wren were cooing like doves at the restaurant until the couple at the next table ordered pheasant under glass. The comparison between people in love and cooing doves is a fitting one because turtledoves are almost always seen in pairs, they mate for life, and their soft cooing has a loving, contented sound.

The "turtle" in *turtledove* evolved into the Old English *turtle* from the Latin *turtur*. When the ancient Romans listened to the cooing doves, they thought they made a sound that resembled the word *turtur*. Later, in Old English, the final *r* was changed to *l*, giving us *turtul*, which then became *turtle*.

Hundreds of years later, *dove* was added to the word. The addition wasn't really necessary, because to the ancients a *turtur*, or turtle, meant dove. The Bible's Song of Solomon 2:12 confirms this: "The time of singing of birds is come, and the voice of the turtle is heard in our land."

On valentines hundreds of years old, birds, and especially doves, appear as symbols of abiding love and affection. And as late as 1910 people living in the Ozark Mountains still believed that birds started pairing off on February 14.

Love

Has a valentine ever been written without mentioning the word *love*? The original root, *leubh,* meant to be fond of, to care for, and to desire, which shows that love and longing have been around since the dawn of civilization. In the northern Netherlands, the old Frisian word was *luve,* and in Old English, the word was *lufu.* In Middle English, the spelling changed from *lufu* to *love,* and it has been *love* ever since.

Love has been examined, poked at, debated, and argued and written about at great length. Perhaps three of the most discussed characteristics of love are its eternal nature, love at first sight, and its tragic side.

The eternal nature of love is expressed in the Bible, in Song of Solomon 8:7. "Many waters cannot quench love, neither can the floods drown it." The vote was not unanimous. Contrast this with the American poet Edna St. Vincent Millay's (1892–1950) poem "Thursday": "And if I loved you Wednesday, / Well, what is that to you? I do not love you Thursday— / So much is true."

One popular belief among some writers was that those who loved at first sight loved more intensely. Do you agree? When the English poet and playwright Christopher Marlowe (1564–1593) died at the age of twenty-nine, he was working on a long poem about two legendary lovers named Hero and Leander. "Where both deliberate, the love is slight, / Whoever loved, that loved not at first sight?" Nearly four hundred years later, the American novelist and short-story writer Carson McCullers expressed quite a different viewpoint on love at first sight in her 1961 book *Clock without Hands*. "In early youth, love at first sight, that epitome of passion, turns you into a zombie."

Perhaps two of the most famous lines ever penned about love are from Alfred Lord Tennyson's (1809–1892) long poem *In Memoriam*: "'Tis better to have loved and lost, / Than never to have loved at all." Tennyson was writing about the death of a best friend, not a sweetheart, who was engaged to marry his sister. It took him seventeen years to finish the poem. A few years after the publication of *In Memoriam* in 1850, the mid-nineteenth-century satirist Samuel Butler offered another interpretation of Tennyson's immortal lines: "'Tis better to have loved and lost / Than never to have lost at all."

Another satirist, Oscar Wilde (1854–1900), wrote about the undeserved pain of loving in his popular novel *The Picture of Dorian Gray*, published in 1891: "Those who are faithless know the pleasures of love; it is the faithful who know love's tragedies."

Pens have gone dry scratching out sentiments on the tragedy of love. Many romantic couples, legendary and real, have died for love. Some poets, like John Dryden (1631–1700), felt it worth the sacrifice, as in these lines from *Conquest of Granada: Part II*: "He who dares love, and for that love / must die / And, knowing this, dares yet love on, am I."

Love vs. Love

....

Pro: To see her is to love her, and love but her for ever,
      For Nature made her what she is, and ne'er made another.
                                      —*Robert Burns*

Con: To be in love is merely to be in a state of perpetual anaesthesis—
      to mistake an ordinary young man for a Greek god or an ordinary
      young woman for a goddess.
                                      —*H. L. Mencken*

Pro: O mother, mother, make my bed,
      O make it soft and narrow:
      My love has died for me to-day,
      I'll die for him to-morrow!

                                      —*Anonymous*

Con: Love has no gift so grateful as his wings.
                                      —*Lord Byron*

Pro: Doubt thou the stars are fire;
      Doubt that the sun doth move;
      Doubt truth to be a liar;
      But never doubt I love.

                                      —*William Shakespeare*

Con: You gave me the key to your heart, my love;
      Then why did you make me knock?
      "Oh, that was yesterday; saints above,
      Last night I changed the lock."
                                      —*John Boyle O'Reilly*

 ## Do You Know?

But how, you may ask, did *love* creep into the game of tennis? Why is having zero points expressed as love? There are two theories on how this happened. The most likely has to do with the nineteenth-century phrase, "to play for love," which today we generally say as "to play for fun," meaning, of course, that there are no, or zero, stakes involved. You play for the pure enjoyment, not for points.

In another theory, the English apparently did not know how to pronounce the French word for egg and/or zero, *l'oeuf* (sounds like luff), so they said *love* instead.

Your serve!

I'd rather eat dirt than
Admire and *Flirt*;
after all, *Bride* and *Groom*
rhyme with doom
and you're better dead
than *Wooed* and *Wed*
because *Marriage* is
for the birds!

Admire

Admire has its roots in the Latin word admirari, which means "to wonder at." This meaning held until the early seventeenth century. You'll find a good example of this use in one of William Shakespeare's (1564–1616) most famous plays. "You have displaced the mirth, / broke the good meeting, / With most admired disorder." (Macbeth, Act III, Scene 4, line 110).

Later, the meaning of admire changed slightly. Not only did you wonder, or marvel, at someone, but you did so with pleasure. It was then flattering to be admired, as it still is today.

Our word mirror comes from the same Latin verb as admire, mirari, "to wonder." After all, don't you gaze into a mirror to indulge in a little self-admiration, or to make yourself look admirable?

Small pieces of mirror were sometimes used on the more expensive and elaborate valentine cards produced during the golden age of valentines, the 1830s to the 1850s. These small bits of mirror indicated a reflective pool in an idyllic landscape. A large piece of mirror could be glued in the center of the card, sometimes under a fabric flap, so that the receiver could admire the image of the one loved by the sender. The accompanying message went something like: "Here you will find the one I love."

 **Do You Know?**

The Greek philosopher Aristotle (384–322 B.C.) was one of the first to mention mirrors in his writings. These early mirrors were not made of glass but were lined with reflective metal. Mirrors as we know them today were first produced in the sixteenth century by the Venetians, who are famous for having perfected the art of glass blowing.

Flirt

The origins of *flirt* are a mystery. Until the middle of the eighteenth century, *flirt* was in common usage as a verb meaning "to throw or move with a jerky movement," as in this observation from the Earl of Dorset, written in 1665: "Perhaps permit some happier man / To kiss your hand or flirt your fan." Nearly one hundred years later, the Scottish novelist Tobias Smollett used *flirt* to describe a brisk sudden motion and, coincidentally, paired it with fan once again. "She flirted her fan with such a fury."

We can only speculate about how *flirt* developed its more amorous side. In one fanciful interpretation, several suitors were courting a young widow in the park on a warm day in mid-eighteenth-century London. The much-admired widow fanned herself as she sat. A nearby matron, taking this all in, claimed the widow was jerking her fan nervously back and forth, while casting flitting—and encouraging—glances from one man to the other. Perhaps the young woman was just trying to keep cool—or perhaps, even more likely, the interfering matron was a bit jealous. Nonetheless, the woman accused the widow of flirting with her fan. Word soon spread among London society, and *flirt* was established as a word synonymous with the act of casually trifling with someone's affections.

A more probable origin of *flirt* is the Old French *fleureter*, to flit from flower to flower (as do bees), hence to utter sweet nothings or to touch lightly. Indeed, isn't this what a flirt does?

By the 1800s, *flirt* had a permanent niche in the standard vocabulary of love and courtship. The Victorian novelist George Eliot, writing in her first full-length novel, *Adam Bede*, nicely summed up the universal attitude toward flirting: "Every man likes to flirt with a pretty girl, and every pretty girl likes to be flirted with."

Bride and Groom

Bride, from the Old English word *bryd*, has always meant a woman just married or about to be married. In Shakespeare's most famous love tragedy, Juliet's father, Capulet, tells his daughter's determined suitor, Paris, that he is not anxious for Juliet to rush to the altar: "My child is yet a stranger in the world; / She hath not seen the change of fourteen years; / Let two more summers wither in their pride, / Ere we may think her ripe to be a bride." (*Romeo and Juliet*, Act I, Scene 2, line 11).

A *bride* can also be something you have a strong affection for, as in Eliza Cook's *Rover's Song*: "The ocean's my home and my bark [sailing ship] is my bride."

It was a custom during wedding feasts in early England to drink a special ale called "bride ale," from *bryd* plus *ealu*, "ale." These two words became *bridal*. Bridal thus came to mean the wedding feast, and later, in the Middle Ages, it referred to the marriage ceremony itself.

The history of the word *groom* is not quite as clear. In ancient times, *groom* was a term used to describe someone who performed menial tasks of any kind, not just taking care of horses. During this time newly married men were expected to wait on their brides at the table, and one theory has it that since these men were acting like servants, or grooms, they then became known as the bride's groom, or the bridegroom.

Another theory is not quite so romantic but has more of a foundation in the actual evolution of the word. The Old English word for *bridegroom* was *brydguma*, *guma* being a man. In Middle English the word became *bridgome*. *Groom* incorrectly but popularly replaced *guma*, and *guma* later disappeared from the language.

One hundred years ago, handsome valentines could cost a week's or more wages, so gentlemen suitors gave serious thought to sending them. Many times the man had marriage on his mind. In this case, the valentine verse would include a suggestive little ditty like:

> Pray, never let us love divide,
> In life or death to faith incline.
> Then come to me, a lovely bride
> To bless thy faithful Valentine.

Suitors pursuing a widow might not be so bold or flowery:

> If it is in the book of fate,
> That you should have another mate,
> I wish your second spouse to be.

Do You Know?

Bride means something quite different to a lepidopterist, someone who specializes in the study of butterflies and moths. The beautiful dark crimson underwing moth is also called a bride. So if you meet someone who tells you they've just netted a bride, you might pause a moment before you accuse them of being a barbarian.

Woo and Wed

Woo carried not a blush of romance in its original meaning, coming from the Old English word *wogian*, which means "to be inclined toward." Later, probably after 1200, *wogian* evolved to *wowen*, then *woo*. Also at that time the definition expanded to specifically mean "to court," with an eye toward marriage.

When a young man wooed a woman in Anglo-Saxon times—roughly until the eleventh century, when the Normans invaded England—he was most likely courting the spouse already selected for him by his parents. Even though the marriage was prearranged, the young man still had to make his intentions known to the bride-to-be's father. This involved going to her father and making a formal pledge.

This Anglo-Saxon pledge, or the stated matrimonial intention, was called a *wedd*. As the custom of requiring a formal engagement, or betrothal, waned, the *wedd* came to mean the actual marriage ceremony, the *wedd*-ing.

When formal pledges of *wedd* were made, the young woman's father gave the prospective husband money or property as a sign of good faith and intentions. This form of material dowry was known as *wedlock*, from the words *wedd*, "pledge," plus *lac*, "offering a gift." So, in early times, wedlock occurred *before* the couple was actually married!

For hundreds of years, eager suitors have sent valentine greetings to woo sweethearts in the hope of getting wed. In fact, from the late eighteenth century to the end of the nineteenth century, sending a valentine to a woman on February 14 was often looked upon as the equivalent of a marriage proposal.

Documented evidence indicates that Margaret Brew, a determined English mother, used Saint Valentine's Day in 1477 as an excuse to play matchmaker for her daughter. She wrote to an eligible bachelor, John Paston, urging him to approach her husband to set the wedding date. The letter is addressed to "right well-beloved Valentine John Paston Esq.":

> upon Friday is St. Valentine's Day and every bird chooseth him a mate, and if it like you to come on Thursday at night, and so purvey you that you may abide there till Monday, I trust to God that you shall speak to my husband, and I shall pray that we shall bring the matter to a conclusion.

The story has a happy ending, thanks to a persistent matchmaking mother:

> At Mom Brew's urgings true,
> John Paston did ardently woo,
> Why, yes, her daughter said,
> Alas, they were happily wed.

Marriage

Although plans leading up to the marriage ceremony don't always develop smoothly, the history of the word *marriage* evolved in an orderly fashion, from the Latin *maritare*, to the Old French and Middle English *mariage*, all meaning "to marry."

The meaning of the word *marriage* has remained the same, but the customs surrounding the ceremony have changed throughout the ages.

During a marriage ceremony in ancient Rome, the bride wore white, symbolizing joy. However, the bridal veil was a bright orange color that suggested the flame of passionate love.

It was the custom for brides in the Victorian era to wear their best finery, in any color, on their wedding day. If, on the other hand, a Victorian bride did wear white it meant that her family was wealthy enough to buy a dress that she would wear for only one day.

The custom of the groom's carrying his bride over the threshold, which came to us from the ancient Mediterranean region, has a curious and somewhat ironic twist. Originally, some social historians put forth the notion that this tradition grew out of either a chivalrous gesture on the part of the male or a custom that indicated the "capture" of his woman. On the contrary. In these early societies, brides were considered powerful figures, and doorways were looked upon as important places, since people believed threatening spirits lived at entryways. In order to appease these spirits, the all-powerful woman allowed herself to be taken across the threshold in a passive position.

Do You Know?

Why do fathers of the bride give their daughters away? Historically, brides were sold by their fathers. As late as the 1880s in England, twelve women were sold as wives for eighteen pence and a glass of beer. Today, it's still the custom for fathers to give the bride away, although in the United States no money changes hands.

June is considered a favorable month in which to marry because June is named after Juno, the goddess of fertility and marriage. And you thought it was because the weather is usually charming in June!

Yet, my *Heart* felt a tug
when you gave me a *Hug*.
I wondered if your *Kiss*
would bring perfect *Bliss*.

Heart

From the Old English *heorte* and, later, the Middle English *hert* comes the word at the center of all valentines *heart*.

Anatomically speaking, in the vertical scheme, the heart is at the body's center, though it is slanted toward the left—which is why you place your right hand on the left side of your chest when you say the Pledge of Allegiance.

When the Egyptians mummified their dead for burial, they removed every organ but the heart. They believed the heart was the only part of the body necessary for the trip through eternity. And, when we talk about the very center of our being, the source of our emotions, we refer to the heart.

Hearts in love have always wavered back and forth, from a state of wild joy to sadness and brokenheartedness. In fact, there's a heart for just about every fate, as Lord Byron (1788–1824) wrote in a letter from the year 1817:

> Here's a sign to those who love me,
> And a smile to those who hate;
> And whatever sky's above me,
> Here's a heart for every fate.

Although the down side of love preoccupies many poets and writers, Christina Rossetti (1830–1894) took a lighter tone in her poem "A Birthday":

My heart is like a singing bird
Whose nest is in a watered shoot;
My heart is like an apple-tree
Whose boughs are bent with thick-set fruit.

Alfred Lord Tennyson reminded us of the heart's vulnerable, fragile state when he wrote in *In Memoriam:* "Never morning wore / To evening, but some heart did break."

There are a host of phrases in which the word *heart* appears. One of the most famous is "heart of heart," which is mistakenly written or spoken as "heart of hearts." Shakespeare originated the expression in *Hamlet*, Act III, Scene 2, line 79:

Give me that man
That is not passion's slave, and I will wear him
In my heart's core, aye, in my heart of heart,
As I do thee.

Here are a few more phrases with *heart*. How many more can you name?

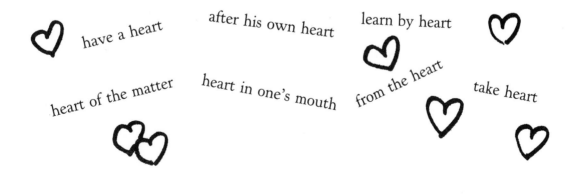

have a heart

after his own heart

learn by heart

heart of the matter

heart in one's mouth

from the heart

take heart

Hug and Kiss   smooch!

Hug is another word with fuzzy beginnings. It may have roots in the early Icelandic word *hugga,* "to comfort." In the late sixteenth century, people were already using *hug* in the sense of a comforting embrace, as in this Shakespearean line: "He bewept my Fortune, and Hugg'd me in his arms." (*Richard III,* Act I, Scene 4, line 252).

Valentines at the turn of the century might have courted in a buggy that had a very narrow seat, barely big enough for two. It was called a "hug-me-tight" buggy. During this same time, women wore short, close-fitting jackets referred to as "hug-me-tights." It seems that these Victorian valentines didn't give themselves much breathing space!

Kiss, on the other hand, has a very definite word history. It comes from the Old English word *cyssan.* In Old Frisian, a kiss is *kessa.* In Old Norse, when you caress someone on the lips, you *koss* them. Some scholars of word histories maintain that the word *kiss* evolved from the sound the lips made when puckering up to deliver a smooch. Listen next time you get or give a kiss.

Did you ever wonder how this whole business of kissing got started? Anthropologists (scientists who study different cultures) have put forth several theories. According to one theory, kissing began when ancient peoples, believing that the

air that left their mouths had magical powers, kissed one another so that their souls might mingle.

Another, more likely theory suggests that kissing on the
mouth evolved from infant and animal impulses. Animals touch
continually. On your last trip to the zoo, you might have
noticed this, especially when you were watching the monkeys.
To express affection, monkeys groom one another, birds stroke
beaks, elephants intertwine their trunks, and cats clean one
another.

Did you ever make an X for *kiss* next to your signature on a letter? The custom of putting an X next to your name goes back to early Christian times and had no connection with romantic kissing. In those days, whenever people signed an important document, they put the cross of Saint Andrew after their name to imply their sincerity. Saint Andrew was one of the twelve apostles, and the cross he was crucified on looks a lot like our letter X. X is also the first letter of the Greek word for Christ, *Xristos*. Signers were further required to kiss the document as a pledge of good faith, much like kissing the Bible. Over time, people continued to use an X after their name, but the religious connotation slowly dissolved. Today, X means a smooch.

During World War II, both the British and American governments prohibited people in their armed forces from adding an X—or two or three—when signing letters to loved ones, for fear military spies would try to use these "kisses" as a way of sending secret messages.

Soldiers couldn't send kisses, and men in early seventeenth-century America were forbidden to kiss a woman in public, even if the woman were their wife. Poor John Kemble of Boston got carried away after returning from a three-year sea voyage and gave his wife a kiss when they met at the dock. He was sentenced to sit for two hours in the stocks. Despite his three-year absence, the homesick John Kemble's conduct was considered "lewd and unseemly."

Did You Know?

Kissing games such as Spin the Bottle and Post Office have been around for centuries. No one knows who invented them or even why. One psychologist has theorized that by playing these games, youngsters who may be too shy to kiss a person of the opposite sex are allowed to experiment. And since chance dictates whom you must kiss, no one can say that you took the initiative with that person.

The Romans were such fans of kissing that they had three different words for it, depending on whom you kissed—an acquaintance (*basium*), a close friend (*osculum*), or a lover (*savium*).

Bliss

The Old English word *bliss* or *bliths* is the source of a favorite valentine word, *bliss*. In its original definition, *bliss* meant "happiness." Yet how often do you say, I'm not very blissful today?

Although no one knows for certain, it's possible that because *bliss* and *bless* are spelled similarly, the religious associations of *bless* may have rubbed off on *bliss*. Thus *bliss* came to mean joy of an ecstatic, heavenly nature. This association is ironic since the origins of the word *bless* are linked to blood, coming from the Old English *blod*, "a bloody sacrifice." Today the French word *blesser*, which means "to wound," still has this violent connection.

Writers have used *bliss* for centuries to describe an elevated state of rapture between people in love. "Eternity was in our lips and eyes, / Bliss in our brows' bent." (William Shakespeare, *Antony and Cleopatra*, Act I, Scene 3, line 36).

An old, faded parchment valentine from 1669 bears this tender sentiment from a poem called "To Dorinda":

> Shall only you and I forbear
> To meet and make a happy pair?
> Shall we alone delay to live?
> This day an age of bliss may give.

When Alfred Lord Tennyson's best friend died in 1833, he wrote *In Memoriam* in his honor. In it he observed, "A wither'd violet is her bliss."

Valentines produced during the nineteenth century were positively dripping with lofty words of romance. Happiness wasn't good enough; lovers felt bliss. Here are some other examples of exaggerated words of love that were popular during the last century.

A Victorian
Valentine Vocabulary

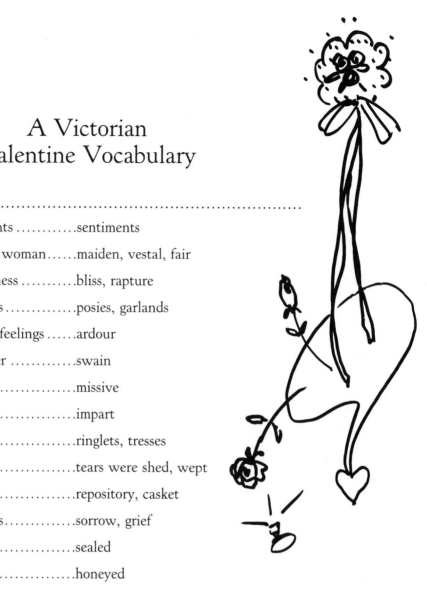

thoughts . . . . sentiments

young woman . . . . . . maiden, vestal, fair

happiness . . . . bliss, rapture

flowers . . . . posies, garlands

warm feelings . . . . . . ardour

admirer . . . . swain

letter . . . . missive

tell . . . . impart

hair . . . . ringlets, tresses

cried . . . . tears were shed, wept

box . . . . repository, casket

sadness . . . . sorrow, grief

closed . . . . sealed

sweet . . . . honeyed

wave . . . . flutter

begin . . . . commence

admire . . . . esteem, endear

innocent . . . . guileless

gift . . . . token, offering

In *Victorian Courtship*
falling in love was a snap;
a *Mushy, Gushy*
Verse on a *Card*,
sweethearts fell in your lap.

Victorian

Whenever we think of elaborate valentine lace confections with flowery verses, the name *Victorian* comes to mind. In Latin, the noun *victory*, with the same root as *Victorian*, is identified with a shout of triumph in battle. The Victorian age proved to be the golden age of valentines, a gentle triumph of romanticism and art.

The Victorian age is named after Queen Victoria, who reigned as queen of Great Britain and Ireland for sixty-five years, from 1837 to 1901, and was empress of India from 1877 to 1901. The first half of her reign was marked by progressive change and exploration, the latter by a rising discontent with moral values and a widening gap between the new science (as championed by Charles Darwin) and religion.

Americans were greatly influenced by the technology, styles, and social customs that drifted across the ocean from Victorian England. By the third decade of the nineteenth century, printers in England, and soon after the United States, had perfected their printing methods and were turning out exquisite embossed papers and die-cut lacy patterns for valentine cards.

Paper was cut, perforated, stamped, embossed, and glazed. Scenes were either painted on paper in watercolor and oils or depicted in lithographs and photographs. The Victorians used unusual materials to ornament these choice tokens, including tiny shells, seaweed, coral, dried grass, precious stones, mother-of-pearl, swansdown, gold and silver bullion, sateen, muslin, velvet, cotton net, rice paper, silk, satin, and even human hair!

We've only to read the descriptions of some of these Victorian valentines to appreciate their high level of refinement:

> "A heart-shaped valentine of cut and embossed silver paper, edged with bright-colored flowers. White net and feathers over a green tulle center make a background for a shell and fillagree-framed medallion portraying a flying Cupid."

It's no wonder people avidly seek out the best of these valentines, and museums and libraries show off prized collections.

 **Do You Know**

Queen Victoria's influence was far-reaching. Her name is used in connection with art, writing, social attitudes, and tastes. In addition, English explorers and naturalists paid homage to their queen by attaching her name to their discoveries and honors.

Do you know that there is a Victoria plum, pigeon, water lily, carriage, cloth, box tree, and Cross?

Victoria is also the capital of British Columbia, the capital of Hong Kong, a state in Australia, a lake in East Africa, a mountain in New Guinea, a waterfall on the border of Zambia and Zimbabwe, an island belonging to Canada, part of Antarctica, and a desert in Australia!

Can you think of any more of Victoria's namesakes? Try looking at a map.

Courtship

The *court* in *courtship* comes from the latin word *cohort*, "a yard or enclosure for livestock." The suffix *-ship* is from the Old English element *-scipe*, which means the quality, state, or condition of something. Isn't it interesting that a word so wedded to romance had its beginnings in a farmyard!

In France, *court*, or *cort*, developed to refer to certain manners and customs in vogue at the French royal court. Later, *cort* was broadened to mean practicing the art of seeking favor not at court but at love. But you can court danger or favors in addition to fair damsels, as in this letter from a firm father.

> Tom: If you make any attempt to court my daughter at the barn dance Saturday night, you'll be courting disaster.
> Sincerely meant,
> Judge Sturgess
> 7th Circuit Court

Thomas Campbell, a nineteenth-century Scottish poet, has advice for those worried about the consequences of their courting: "Better to be courted and jilted / Than never be courted at all." Does this sound familiar?

Mushy and Gushy

Some of our more colorful and descriptive words in English came into the language not from an Old English word or a Latin root, but based on their imitation of a particular sound. These words are said to be echoic, because their pronunciation echoes a particular sound. Another, much longer word for echoic is onomatopoeic, which comes from the Greek *onoma*, "name," and *poiein*, "to make," or, in other words, "the making of a name." Common echoic words include *buzz, hiss, swat, thump, swish, swash*—and *mushy* and *gushy*.

Mushy is derived from the word *mash*. When you mash something, you make it soft and pulpy by applying pressure. In the late nineteenth century, a man who tried to attract a woman's attention—or put pressure on her—was called a masher. And, appropriately, when a masher flirted he was said to go a-mashing.

About the same time, references to *mushy* meaning tender and sentimental were in use. G. Stratton Porter (1863–1924) was an American novelist noted for her sentimental romances. From her book *Laddie* comes: "They formed a circle around Sally and Peter and as mushy as ever they could they sang, 'As sure as the grass grows around the stump, You are my darling sugar lump,' while they danced."

Mushy also refers to something—or someone—lacking in firmness. So, if you're a mush-head you give in to everyone.

Don't be a mush-head and think you have to write mushy verses on Saint Valentine's Day!

Gushy developed from the Middle English words *gosshe* and *gusche* as a way of describing the sound made by a rushing flow of liquid. It extended to include a rush of words expressing an excessive outpouring of tenderness. In *Nancy,* a book by Miss Broughton, one rejected gusher tells us: "I go to bed, feeling rather small, as one who has gushed, and whose gush has not been welcome to the recipient." The famous nineteenth-century English writer and critic John Ruskin (1819–1900) felt the same way about people who overpraised works of art. "There were few things I hated more than hearing people gush about particular drawings."

Do you tend to gush when you hear love mush?

Verse

Both the Old French and Old English word *vers* come from the Latin *versus*, which means "a turning." Roman farmers called their furrows *versus*, since at the end of each row, they "turned" their work animal around and went back to the beginning. It's thought that at some point, someone observed that reading a poem was a little like plowing a field: once you get to the end of the line, you turn around and go back to the beginning. Lines of poetry then became known as *verses*. Later, the term was applied to the entire stanza.

We have few examples of valentine verses written as early as the fourteenth century. The following verse, a rare exception, is believed to be one of the oldest to mention Saint Valentine. The writer reveals his own name in the last line. We can only speculate as to why a friar calls himself a valentine! The poem is written in Middle English. See if you can figure out the words.

> Thow it be alle other wyn
> Godys blescing have he and myn,
> My none gentyl Volontyn,
> Good Tomas the frere.

Translation:
> Though it be all other wine,
> God's blessing have he and mine,
> My none gentle Valentine,
> Good Thomas the friar.

51

Friar Thomas may be the first valentine to mention the patron saint of lovers, but the distinction of sending the first rhymed valentine goes to the French poet Charles, Duke of Orleans. The duke was held prisoner in the Tower of London in 1415 after the French lost the Battle of Agincourt.

With plenty of time on his hands, Charles used the opportunity to send his wife early valentines called "poetical," or amorous, addresses. One went like this. (Bear in mind that Charles wrote mostly in Norman-French. This verse, which has been modernized, seems surprisingly contemporary.)

> Wilt thou be mine? dear love, reply,—
> Sweetly consent, or else deny;
> Whisper softly, none shall know,—
> Wilt thou be mine, love? ay or no?

The next century, the sixteenth, is rich in valentine verse. Lancelot Andrewes, one of Queen Elizabeth I's (1533–1603) favorite chaplains and a preparer of the King James version of the Bible, wrote this valentine. One can only conclude that his sweetheart was a great animal lover.

> I bear in sign of love
> A sparrow in my glove,
> And in my breast a dove,
> This shall be all thine:
> Besides of sheep a flock
> Which yieldeth many a lock,
> And this shall be thy stock:
> Come, be my Valentine!

The superstition, prevalent from the early 1600s on, that you would marry the first person you saw on Saint Valentine's Day is echoed in Shakespeare's *Hamlet* (Act IV, Scene 5, line 50) when Ophelia sings: "Tomorrow is Saint Valentine's day, / All in the morning betime, / And I a maid at your window, / To be your Valentine."

Most valentines did not have Shakespeare's flair for poetic phrasing. For them, help arrived in the form of Valentine Writers, which were first published in England in the early 1700s before being imported to the colonies. These little booklets contained rhymes tailored for everyone, from a blacksmith to a milkmaid. They even included answers for verse-tied receivers to send back.

This sample addresses a very specific situation.

> A short time since I danc'd with you,
> And from that hour lov'd you true;
> Your pleasing form, your charming air,
> Might with a fabl'd grace compare—

If you wanted to encourage this gentleman who danced with you, you might feel inclined to send this answer from the Valentine Writer.

> Your Valentine is very kind,
> Nor did a cool reception find;
> Your company gave me delight,
> When I danced with you t'other night;
> Then mutually we did incline,
> Our hearts to love, my Valentine

Well, you might ask, what if I don't want to encourage the man who sent me a mushy valentine? Valentine Writers offered discouraging responses, too, as this one in *Cupid's Annual Charter*, from 1810.

Valentine

I love and court a fond return,
My breast it does with ardour burn;
I hope you feel an equal flame,
And burn with ardour just the same,
The fire of love consumes my heart,
Hasten comfort to impart;
Your consent would to me prove,
A healing balsam my dear love,
With rapture I'd receive a line,
From thee my dearest Valentine.

Answer

Your Valentine so full of flame,
I put into the fire;
Against your folly I exclaim,
Such nonsense all must tire
As I had neither twine or rope,
I could not send a line,
But if you wish to hang, I hope
You'll buy one, Valentine.
But as you're full of raging fire,
Water would better cool,
So take a leap off London Bridge,
And drown yourself, poor fool.

The highly decorative lace paper valentines of the nineteenth century had few equals in lavishness—nor did their verses for creaky, high-blown sentimentality. This valentine verse, sent to Miss Emma Drinker of Wooster Street in New York City in 1845, typifies rhymes of the period. This one is particularly interesting because it's apparent from the rather obvious crossing out of "Mary" that the sender wanted to offend Emma, who must have hurt (or smashed) his tender feelings.

To Emma

Go little card to ~~Mary~~ Emma
ever dear. Breathe the warm
sign and shed a tear.
To tell her how much I love and to
her impart
The tender feelings of a
broken heart.
Thy memory is dear to me.

Toward the end of the nineteenth century, comic valentines were all the rage. Often cruel in tone, they poked fun at old maids and people in various professions. This comic valentine from the Civil War period indicates some resistance on the part of the soldier's sweetheart.

A Regular

My love is a regular man—
A man with a regular way;
He means to regulate me—if he can,
When he gets his regular pay.
But I'll be no regular's wife,
No! no! not for all creation;
For who could enjoy married life,
When bound to a mere regulation.

Twentieth-century verse saw a return to sentimental verses, but silly rhymes, like this one, remain popular.

Everytime you look at me
My heart goes pitter-patter
But for heaven's sake
Don't look that way,
Unless I really matter.

Valentine Writers are no longer produced, so here is a partially completed valentine greeting to help get you into the poetic swing of valentine timing and rhyming.

Shall only you and I _____,
To meet and make a happy _____,
Shall we alone delay to _____,
This day an age of bliss may _____.

Suggested word list: confess, mess, find, bind, dare, pair, roam, home, marry, tarry

56

Card

The word *card* goes back to the Latin *charta* and the Greek *chartēs*, meaning a papyrus leaf. *Charta* developed in Middle French as *carte*, perhaps from Old Italian *carta*, a "sheaf of paper." It's a puzzle as to how the English word ended up as *card*, since it came into the Scottish language as *carte*.

The first valentine greetings were not cards as we know them today but simply large sheets of paper. The paper had no decoration other than the ink, which, like the paper, may have been colored. When Mrs. Samuel Pepys, the wife of the celebrated English diary keeper Samuel Pepys, received a valentine from little Will Mercer in London, on February 14, 1667, it consisted simply of her name written in gold letters on a piece of pretty blue paper.

In this country, the history of the valentine card began during the middle of the eighteenth century. Simple but artistic, these handmade greetings featured original verses and were delivered by hand, after first being folded and sealed with red wax. With more leisure time, these early valentine senders spent hours on their cards, which took the form of watercolors, pinpricks, cutouts, rebuses, love knots, and acrostics.

Do You Know?

Acrostic is a Greek word which comes from two roots: *akros,* "topmost" or "highest," and *stichos,* "a line of verse." An acrostic therefore refers to a line of verse in which certain letters in each line, usually the first or last, when read in sequence, spell out a name.

This American acrostic, which contains some pretty antiquated, formal language, dates from 1760:

> All hail fair vestal, lovely gift of heaven,
> Nourished in prudence and in wisdom given.
> Neglect not this small present from a friend,
> Esteem commences where fierce passions end.
> Transcendent Fair resplendent star approve
> His pleading reasons who thus seeks your love,
> Accept his proffers, take his heart in care.
> Cherish his passion in a modest sphere.
> How then will heaven our constancy commend.
> Empyreal bounties happy moments send,
> Refulgent blisses crown us to our end.

Across the middle of the valentine is written: "Join the first letter of each line you'll find, / How sweet the name, how perfect and how kind." (The first letters of each line together spell the name Anne Thacher.)

Commercial valentines first appeared in England around 1800, when printmakers issued sentimental illustrations and verses in engravings and woodcuts. The golden age of valentines, from 1830 to 1850, brought exquisite lace papers decorated with mirrors, beads, feathers, and shells. Some cards were shaped like fans, others had windows that opened, some were mechanical and had moving parts. Early cards included a blank place on which senders either wrote an original verse or, if they needed help from the poetic muse, picked one they liked from a Valentine Writer.

The best valentines in the United States before 1850 all came from England and cost up to fifty dollars apiece. Crudely hand-colored American woodcut greetings were no match for the elegantly romantic Victorian valentines. But in 1849 in Worcester, Massachusetts, an enterprising young woman named Esther Howland began to produce valentines in English fashion. She imported fine papers and decorations and turned the third floor of her house into an all-female valentine assembly line. In 1857 valentine enthusiasts bought up three million valentines in the United States alone and, in the process, firmly established the American greeting-card industry.

Within twenty years, however, imitation lace paper, poorly printed verses, and cheap penny postcard greetings with vulgar sentiments (called vinegar valentines) ushered in the end of the romantic era of valentines. By the Gay Nineties, cards were garish, fringed, and cheap-looking. An item from the

Daily News in 1898 reads, "The Christmas card (which evolved after the valentine) has apparently killed the valentine. . . . They are still sold, and sent, but they are chiefly of the satirical order." In Chicago in the late 1890s, the post office rejected some twenty-five thousand valentines on the grounds they were not fit to be carried through the mails.

Although sending valentines in England died out by World War I, valentine makers in the United States continued to churn out cards despite paper shortages and a decline in sales. The custom was kept alive thanks primarily to schoolchildren who set up valentine boxes in their classrooms. And some say it was the homesick American soldiers stationed in England during World War II who renewed English interest in Cupid's greetings, when they urged English shopkeepers to sell valentines for them to mail to loved ones in the United States.

 **Do You Know?**

Did you ever hear someone refer to a person as being a "card"? Such a person is amusing and usually a little eccentric or peculiar. This descriptive adjective evolved from the game of playing cards itself. The novels of Charles Dickens (1812–1870) are full of many memorable cards, such as Krook in *Bleak House*. "You know what a card Krook was for buying all manner of old pieces of furniture."

Make Your Own
Old-Fashioned Valentine Card

Endless Knot of Love

A true Love Knot, or Endless Knot of Love, valentine was very popular both in England and America in the seventeenth century. The sweet sentiments on these love knots had no beginning or end, which meant they could be read from any line and still make sense. Use this drawing as a guide. Then try to make up your own messages and write them in each link of the knot. Make sure you can read the lines randomly from any point on the knot.

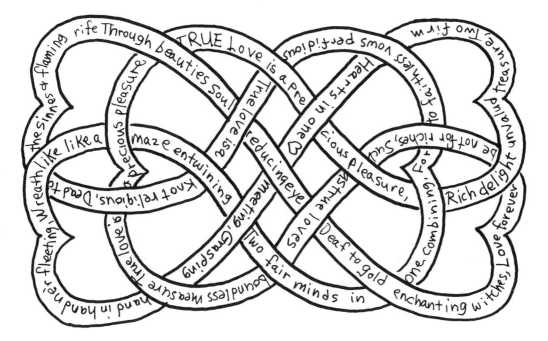

Pinprick

The Pennsylvania Dutch, descendants of the German immigrants who settled in central Pennsylvania in the early eighteenth century (*Duutsch* in Middle Dutch meant German), introduced several lovely art forms, among them the pinprick. You can easily make a pinprick valentine of your own. Trace a pretty valentine design (such as hearts, birds, or flowers) onto tracing paper. Cut a valentine card to size, preferably from a white or beige sheet of good quality watercolor paper with a high rag content. Lay the tracing paper over the card and with a straight pin "trace" the lines of the design by pricking small holes close together onto the rag paper. For a special effect, first dip the pin into colored inks or food coloring. Pinprick designs look especially attractive when held up to a light.

Rebus

Some of the oldest handmade valentines in collections today are rebuses. *Rebus* is a Latin word which means "things" or, more accurately, "that which is indicated by things." A rebus is a kind of puzzle or riddle, and the words are indicated by pictures. Here's an easy valentine rebus to get you started. Can you invent others?

(answer: be mine)

62

Embossed Heart

The most elegant examples of Victorian paper valentines and envelopes from the mid-nineteenth century most often included embossing. When printmakers emboss, they use metal plates and chemicals. However, you can fashion embossed cards with ordinary, inexpensive materials. First cut out a heart or other decorative valentine shape from a piece of board (such as cardboard or bristol board from an art supply store). The thicker the board, the more raised your embossing will be. Glue the shape onto another piece of stiff cardboard. Then cut your valentine card to the size you want from a piece of heavy watercolor paper. Lay the paper over your design, making sure it is in proper position. Using a crochet hook, gently but firmly rub over the outline of the cutout design, pushing down on the hook until the paper begins to raise up. Afterward you can add a verse in ink or a pale wash of watercolor.

Jigsaw Puzzle

If you want your friends to "puzzle over" your message, try making a valentine jigsaw. Draw an original design, write a poem on a piece of cardboard, or glue already printed illustrations onto the board. Cut the design or poem into several pieces (a heart-shaped piece in the center might be fun), and touch up the edges with clear nail polish. Drop the pieces into an envelope and send to your heart's delight for unscrambling.

Acrostic

A valentine acrostic is a fine challenge, especially for those who like to write. Compose romantic verses, arranging them so that the first letter of each line when read downward spells out the name of your valentine. Tell him or her somewhere on the card what you've done. Then be sure you send it to the *right* person!

So, I sent my *Dear Sweetheart*
Chocolate,
a *Rival Swashbuckler* sent
Silk, *Satin*, and *Lace*.
Alas, my *Red Rose* and love *Letter*
were thrown in my face.

Dear

The Old English word *deore* and, later, the Middle English *dere* evolved to give us our word *dear*. The modern spelling appeared in the 1500s, shortened from "dear one" and "my dear." The original meaning conveyed feelings of esteem and value rather than love specifically, but the word soon became synonymous with affection.

Dear was used as a form of address as early as 1450. The English dramatist William Congreve first made use of the interjection "oh dear!" in 1694 in his play *The Double Dealer*. The exclamation "dear me!" turns up in 1773 in Oliver Gold-smith's play *She Stoops to Conquer*. As the opposite of cheap, dear entered the vocabulary as early as the eleventh century.

Consider the many different ways we use the word today:

> My dear Horatio, Dear me! When I did not hear from you for so long, I began to worry dearly. Then, oh, dear! Such a surprise came by this morning's post. The cameo, which must have cost you dear, shall remain one of my dearest and most cherished possessions.
>
> Your dearest betrothed, Emily.

The Old English *deore* evolved to form *deorling*, which became *derling* in the Middle English and then *darling*. *Dearest* and *darling* are two favorite words for valentines. Can you think of any others?

Sweetheart

From the two Old English words *swete* and *heorte* we get *sweetheart*. In the Middle Ages *sweetheart* was often written as two words, as in the poet Geoffrey Chaucer's 8,239-line poem *Troilus and Criseyde*, "For-yeue it me myn owene swete herte."

In American slang, *sweetheart* is also used when referring to something especially good; for example, a car salesman might comment, "What a sweetheart of an automobile." In contrast, the word so associated with lovers and quality is also used in an ironic sense. Did you ever see an old movie on television in which Humphrey Bogart or Edward G. Robinson said, "Start talking, sweetheart, or I'll plug you full of lead"? He was most likely talking to someone named Fast Eddie Magee, not to his girlfriend!

Another popular term of endearment is *honey*, which comes to us from the Old English word *hunig*. In the Middle English period, *hunig* evolved to *hony*. "The Miller's Tale," one of the stories from Chaucer's *The Canterbury Tales*, written during the 1390s, tells a story about Alison, a young woman in love with a handsome scholar. She is lovingly called "Alisoun his hony deere." That's really piling on the sweet sentiments!

Another and somewhat old-fashioned word used to express tenderness is *sugarplum*. Everyone has heard of sugarplum fairies, but did you know that there is a real candy called a sugarplum? Sugarplums are made by boiling sugar, adding flavoring and coloring, and shaping while warm into oval or round shapes. Many a sweetheart in the seventeenth and eighteenth centuries received sugarplums from their dear hearts. In the nineteenth century, *sugarplum* was even used as a verb to indicate a pampered and petted person: "At present, pretty dear, she is coaxed and sugar-plumbed through life."

Other love greetings over the years incorporated members of the animal and plant kingdoms. You might have greeted your love with, Hello my sweet: pigeon, lamb, pea, cabbage, duck, goose, and, as we have seen earlier, turtledove.

Chocolate

If you stepped up to a candy counter on Saint Valentine's Day and asked for a box of *cacauatl*, what do you think you would get? Probably nothing but a confused stare. You should, however, get a box of chocolates, for *cacauatl* is the Mexican word for cacao, the bean from which chocolate is made.

When the Spanish, led by Hernando Cortez, invaded Mexico in 1519, they were introduced to a cold chocolate drink made from the cacao bean. The drink, made by both the Aztecs and the Mayans, was called *cacauatl*. But the Spaniards mistakenly called it *chocolatl*, a food the Indians ate. When Cortez wrote back to his king, Charles I of Spain, he reported, "*Chocolatl* is the divine drink that builds up resistance and fights fat." The caffeine in the chocolate drink no doubt accounted for his men's stamina. As far as fighting fat, well, the Mexican version of cold chocolate was sugar-free.

The Spanish felt the puckery brew could be improved upon, so they added sugar and served it hot. The first hot chocolate was served in Spain, where it was a big hit. The English enjoyed it, too, according to Samuel Pepys, who noted in an entry in his diary dated November 24, 1664: "To a coffee-house, to drink jocolatte, very good."

Do You Know?

The United States consumes 21 percent of the world's chocolate and cocoa products. The average citizen eats about three-and-a-half pounds of chocolate a year. In 1990, sweet-tooth valentines in the United States bought up over 600 million dollars worth of chocolates and candy.

The Necco Company makes 1.7 billion pastel conversation hearts every year. That many hearts placed back to back would reach from Boston to San Francisco and back to New York. Some of the most popular hearts say "I love you," "Kiss me," and "Dream boat."

Rival

As the capital and center of the vast Roman Empire, Rome was a highly civilized city. From Rome sprang an organized system of laws and government. Yet despite this high degree of order, the Romans failed to set up any laws governing fishing and hunting. In other words, territories were not established and there was no game warden to settle disputes. As a result, the Romans were continually squabbling over rights to fish in the streams and hunt in the forests. Many arguments ended in death.

In Latin a *rivus* was a "stream or brook." During Roman times, if you lived near or fished the same stream as someone else you were referred to as a *rivalis*. Since these Roman fishermen were very often at odds over fishing rights, the English borrowed the term and dropped the final *-is* to become *rival*. The English used the word to indicate opponents who fought over anything—halibut or hearts!

In a medieval Celtic legend, King Arthur of the famous Round Table had a wife named Guinevere. She was torn between her love for her husband and her love for his most valiant knight, Launcelot. King Arthur and Launcelot are well-known rivals in love. Can you think of any others?

Swashbuckler

Like mushy and gushy, *swashbuckler* is an echoic, or onomatopoeic, word that evolved from imitating a sound. In medieval times, the *swash* of *swashbuckler* was said to have described the sound of a blow on impact, especially one made by a sword. *Buckler* comes from the Middle French *bocler*, which was a small shield with an embossed ornament on the front.

If while fencing a man repeatedly and deliberately struck his own or his adversary's shield with his sword, he was said to be a swashbuckler for making an unnecessary racket. In other words, he was swashing the buckler, or *swashing* the *bocler*. Some years later, the term broadened to include all show-offs.

Swashbucklers, especially those in movies and books, have always been considered romantic figures. Errol Flynn and Douglas Fairbanks, Jr., who portrayed handsome, daring, and adept swordsmen in the 1930s, were two of the most famous movie swashbucklers.

The most renowned literary swashbucklers are Athos, Porthos, and Aramis, the best swordsmen of their day. Perhaps you know them better by the name they adopted, the Three Musketeers, in the famous historical romance written by the French novelist and dramatist Alexandre Dumas in 1844. There were actually four musketeers. D'Artagnan, the book's main character, aspires to be one of Louis XIII's guardsmen but becomes a musketeer only after he successfully duels with the other three. That's a lot of swashing swordplay!

Silk, Satin, and Lace

These precious, rare materials were coveted by those early valentines eager to make a big hit on February 14.

The origin of the word *silk* is as mysterious as its Far Eastern home. Some word historians believe *silk* first came into the Greek language from the Far East as *serikos*, which is derived from *Seres*, the Greek name for the Chinese, who first discovered silk. The Old English word for *silk*, *seolus*, later became *seolke*, then *selk*, and then around 1300 *silk*.

The word history of *satin* is just as slippery. The Old French word *satin* may have come from the Arabic phrase *atlas zaituni*, or satin of Zaitun. Zaitun was the Arab name for a coastal city in southern China. During the thirteenth-century reign of Kublai Khan, the Venetian explorer Marco Polo described the city of Zaitun (now identified as Chuanchow), as a thriving port. We do know satin fabric reached Europe from China by way of the Middle East, and some believe the glossy silk material may have first been made in or around Zaitun.

In 1780 a young woman might have given her sweetheart

a small piece of silk or satin, on which she had embroidered her name, the date, and a sentimental phrase, such as "Truly Thine." The young man who received this token would put it inside his metal watch case to keep dust out of the works. In return, he might have exhausted his savings to buy her a valentine gift, perhaps silk stockings, satin garters, a fussy lace paper valentine card with a padded satin heart and silk ribbon, or a perfumed satin sachet.

Do You Know?

No one knows for sure how silk was discovered, but according to one story, it all started about four thousand years ago in the palace garden of the Chinese empress Si-Ling-Chi. While strolling under some mulberry trees, she looked up and noticed strange yellow and white cocoons on the twigs. Bending down a branch, she watched with amazement as fat white caterpillars spun cobweb-fine threads around their bodies. The empress unraveled the cocoon and spun together the fibers. Thus the first silk was—or may have been—made. Because of her discovery, the empress Si-Ling-Chi became known as the Goddess of the Silkworm. Her secret was closely guarded for nearly three thousand years, but eventually the silkworms found their way to India and Japan. Or, at least, that is the way this one legend was spun. Perhaps someone "wormed" the secret out of a Chinese silk spinner!

The history of lace begins with the Latin word *laqueus*, a "noose, snare, or trap." *Laqueus* passed into Old French as *laz* and Middle English as *las*. In "The Knight's Tale," one of the stories in *The Canterbury Tales*, Chaucer tells of how "Vulcanus had caught thee in his *las*." *Las* kept its original meaning of noose for a while before evolving to mean a "string or cord for tying." You can still find this meaning today in words like *shoelace*.

Las then developed to include the intricate openwork fabric of fine threads, or *lace*. Lace still carries some of its original Latin meaning. Look carefully at the intricate, spidery openwork in lace fabric. Can you see the maze of loops and knots entangled in its delicate pattern? The same can be said for lace paper used to fashion elegant valentines, which were then sent to "snare" an admirer. And, of course, wedding gowns and veils are traditionally made of fine lace.

The French produced a crude form of lace paper as early as the beginning of the nineteenth century. It consisted of large sheets of writing paper perforated with varying sizes of pinpricked holes. About thirty years later, lace paper making was accidentally discovered in England at a London stationery firm. As it developed over the century, lace paper making became a fine art and lacy valentines from this period, with their scalloped edges and cutout, embossed designs, are prized by today's collectors of old-fashioned, spun-sugar valentines.

By the 1870s in the United States, several firms produced lace paper cards that sold for up to thirty-five dollars apiece.

During this time men usually sent only one valentine to that very special person. As the century came to a close, lace paper valentines changed. No longer delicate, the paper was coarser, glossy, and heavily embossed; as one observer noted, these love tokens were a "jumbled mess, choked by lace and their own excess."

Red Rose

Yes, roses are red, and so are bleeding hearts, padded silk sachets, satin ribbons, heart-shaped candy boxes, and sealing wax on old-fashioned valentines. Yet for a color so bound to love, the history of the word *red* has not been, for the most part, a romantic one.

Coming from the Old English word *read*, *red* was, in ancient times, considered the color of honor because it is the color of blood—the vital fluid of human beings. For this reason, ecclesiastical robes were always a deep crimson red. Later, in the early eighteenth century, the Catholic church used red letters to indicate saint's days on their calendars, giving us the phrase a "red-letter day," or an important one.

From the fifteenth century on, red also came to represent war and rebellion. Two English houses, York and Lancaster, fought a series of wars between 1455 and 1485 called the Wars of the Roses, which took its name from the emblems of the two houses: a white rose for the Yorks and a red rose for the Lancasters. Rebels overthrowing Louis XVI during the French Revolution, which began in 1789 and lasted ten years, called themselves Red Republicans because they supposedly dipped their hands in the blood of the nobility they executed. Communist Reds took their name from the color of their revolutionary flag, which is now considered the official flag of the Soviet Union.

A century before the Russian Revolution of 1917, a time of quill pens and expensive postage, sending a valentine was considered a luxury. Patient valentine makers glued cupids onto thick, gilt-edged paper, folded the card, and applied a red wax seal. The flowery verse on the valentine might have begun, "Because the rose is red. . . ."

Roses belong to a plant group called *Rosa* in Latin. The Old English word *rose* developed from the Latin word *rosa*. Roses today, of which there are some thirty thousand varieties, symbolize love and, considering their great expense, luxury. Emperor Nero (A.D. 37–68) of Rome was said to have ordered his servants to stuff his pillows with damask rose petals. The phrase "bed of roses" may reflect Nero's luxurious reclining habits, although the phrase first appeared in writings from the early seventeenth century, as in this line from *Emblems*, a book by the English poet Francis Quarles. "He repents in thorns, that sleeps in beds of roses."

Roses do have prickly thorns, and the thorny part of love was often written about in early valentines. This sentimental verse is from the nineteenth century:

> Beneath the Rose a thorn is found,
> Beneath love's smile, a dart,
> May heaven grant, that neither wound
> Thy young and guileless heart.

 **Do You Know?**

Sub rosa is a Latin phrase that means literally "under the rose," or in strict confidence. It's a term you might have heard in reference to legal documents or court procedures. Its origins are unclear, but according to a Greek legend, Cupid, the Roman god of love, handed a rose to Harpocrates, the god of silence. It was a form of hush money, or a bribe, since Cupid then commanded Harpocrates to keep quiet about Venus's many love affairs.

After that the rose became a symbol of silence. In the early sixteenth century, a rose was placed over Catholic confessionals to symbolize the bond of privacy between priest and confessor. In England, a rose hanging from the ceiling in a room indicated that anything said in the room was to be considered secret. "When we desire to confine our words, we commonly say they are spoken under the rose," said Sir Thomas Browne, an English scholar. Today, you can still see rose carvings on the ceilings of medieval English banquet halls.

Letter

Letters conveying messages of love have been the corner-stone of courtships through the ages. We have our word *letter* thanks to the Latin word *littera*, which meant first a letter of the alphabet and then those letters collectively, or a written note. *Littera* evolved in Old French as *lettre* and in Middle English as *letter*.

One of the most unique relics of Elizabethan England (1558–1603) is a poignant love letter from 1599, written by a man suffering the pangs of separation. Note the Elizabethan spellings differ from contemporary spellings, but the words are usually close enough to understand the meaning.

The letter is addressed, To his lovinge frinde, M[istress] Marye Loveringe:

> *O my sweete harte the longe absence of your persone hath constraynede me to expresse unto you my deere, the inwarde griefes, the secrete sorrowes, the pinchinge paynes that my poor oppressed harte pitifullye endureth. My tremblinge hand is scarce able holde the penne, neither dare my stammeringe tongue to expresse that which my afflicted harte desireth to manifest unto you. Therefore, my Sweete, vouchsafe to graunte some speedie remydie unto the grievous anguishes of my hea-vaye harte. . . .*

Any man who didn't snag a sweetheart by Saint Valentine's Day would consider his letters, verses, and gifts truly love's labors lost. Among other virtues, it was critical that courting gentlemen have excellent penmanship. It might seem strange, but the *way* a man wrote was more important than *what* he wrote. Many a young girl's father rejected potential suitors and would not give consent to the marriage if the young man's love letters lacked the proper number of flourishes and scrolls.

 ## Do You Know?

In days gone by, if you came across a packet of old love letters too faded to read, you might have tried an old formula to restore the original lettering. First you would have collected some gallnuts.

Have you ever noticed bumpy swellings on the leaves of plants or on tree trunks? When insects and fungi invade a healthy plant, the tissue reacts by swelling up around the spot where the insects are attacking. The swelling that forms is called a "gall." Galls shaped like nuts are called "gallnuts."

Then, once you had collected the gallnuts—perhaps from an oak tree—you would have boiled them in wine (with your parents' supervision, of course) then steeped a sponge in the liquid and rubbed it over the faded lines of the letter. Like magic the letters would have appeared fresh, and you would have been able to peek at someone's romantic thoughts.

After which, the letter's angry owner might justly have accused you, "You've got a lot of gall!"

My last resort is a *Diamond*.
I'll offer the *Ring* tonight.
If that doesn't work,
there's zero *Romance* in sight.

Diamond

Diamond is one of the many words introduced into our language from the Old French. Many of these words deal with fashion and social life; among them, apparel, taffeta, jewel, dance, and coiffeur.

The word *diamond* can be traced back to the late Latin word *diamas*, which comes from the earlier Latin *adamas*, meaning "the hardest metal." The base of *adamas* is *adamant*, and if you're adamant about something you might be accused of being hard-headed. Diamonds are certainly hard-headed! Around 1325, Old French *diamant* was borrowed into Old English as *diamaunde*. Eventually it was used to refer to the gem itself.

Diamonds have long been favorite love tokens, yet up until the middle of the fifteenth century the gem was associated with royal power, not love. Some historians believe that it was when a mistress of King Charles VII of France (1403–1461) sported a rock from the king that diamonds became officially recognized as "a girl's best friend."

Ever since King Charles's opulent gift, diamonds have proved themselves the ultimate expression of love and devotion. Thanks to the diligent diary keeping of Samuel Pepys, we have a wonderfully accurate picture of English life in the latter half of the seventeenth century. And Pepys never failed to mention

Saint Valentine's Day. Although tight with his money, Pepys splurged on his wife's valentine present in 1668: "As my valentine gift this year gave her a Turkey-stone set with diamonds . . . I am glad of it for it is fit the wretch should have something to content herself with." Bear in mind wretch was at that time considered a term of endearment.

Do You Know

The Venetians were the first to discover the hardness of diamonds and how fine cutting and polishing would release their brilliance. Yet even though diamonds are so hard that they cannot be scratched, they break easily.

Since 1870, over 97 percent of the world's diamonds have come from Africa. The largest diamond ever found is called the "Cullinan," unearthed in the Transvaal, South Africa, in 1905. It weighed 3,106 carats—that's about one-and-one-third pounds!

Here's a list of some of the most famous diamonds.

Great Mogul	Star of the South	Taylor-Burton
Orloff	Jonker	(Who do you think
Koh-i-nor	Tiffany	this diamond is
Shah	Hope	named after?)
Regent	Kimberley	Earth Star

Ring

Our word *ring* evolved from the Old English word *hring*, a "circular band." Because of the difficulty of pronouncing the *hr* combination, the *h* was eventually dropped.

In 1500, if someone asked you to be the ringleader, they would not have wanted you to head up a group of thugs or spies, but they would have expected you to lead the ring, or the dance.

We know from examining the remains in Egyptian tombs that the Egyptians wore decorative rings on their fingers as early as 2800 B.C. But the origins of the wedding ring are disputed.

Some historians feel the circular band symbolized the ring barbarians used to chain their wives to their houses. Certainly a more romantic interpretation involves the custom in Old Kingdom Egypt of exchanging bands at a wedding ceremony. The Egyptians felt the wedding ring signified a circle with no beginning or end, and so represented the eternity of the marriage.

Rings were popular in ancient Italy, too. One two-thousand-year-old ring unearthed at Pompeii shows an engraving of two carved hands clasped in a handshake. This same design is commonly used on friendship rings today.

In A.D. 860 Pope Nicholas I decreed that an engagement ring was an absolute requirement if people intended to marry. He also indicated the ring had to be fashioned of a valuable metal, preferably gold. The pope felt the husband-to-be should make a financial sacrifice in buying the ring. Thus a tradition was born! By the seventeenth century, the diamond had become the most popular stone in Europe for marking engagements, and certainly the diamond's popularity has not faded.

For centuries, rings have proved popular gifts on Saint Valentine's Day. In mid-seventeenth-century London, Lord Mandeville bestowed on his valentine, a Miss Stuart, a ring that cost about three hundred pounds, the equivalent of about five hundred dollars today. Miss Stuart also received a ring from a former valentine that cost eight hundred pounds! Sounds like Miss Stuart's old flame (the one who drew her name in the valentine lottery the previous year) was trying to make more of an impression than the new one.

Do You Know?

Perhaps the youngest female ever to become engaged—and in the process receive history's smallest engagement ring—was Princess Mary, the daughter of King Henry VIII of England. She was two years old when she became engaged in 1518 to the son of the French king, Francis I, as a way of cementing relations between the two countries. So much for romance! The marriage, however, did not take place.

Romance

Did you ever see an old movie called *Three Coins in the Fountain*? It's about three young American women who go to Rome, the eternal city, searching for eternal romance. And they all find it. Far-fetched Hollywood? Well, from the word-history point of view, romance did, in fact, set down its tangled roots in Rome.

The word *romance* evolved in Latin from *Roma*, "Rome," to *Romanicus*, "of the Roman language or people," to the Old French *romanz escrire*, which means "to write in a Romance language," and on to the English *romance*.

The Romance languages are composed of seven groups of languages that all have Latin as their basis. These languages include French, Italian, Spanish, and Portuguese. The common people in ancient Rome spoke what is referred to as Vulgar Latin, an informal speech, as opposed to the classical Latin of the more educated. Most language experts agree that Vulgar Latin is the chief source of the Romance languages. (And, of course, our word *vulgar* means common.)

Medieval romances were tales written primarily in French verse about brave heroes like King Arthur, Charlemagne, and Alexander the Great. The notion of having a romance with another person is thought to have developed sometime during the Middle Ages in reference to the chivalric love depicted in these medieval romances.

In the late eighteenth century and on through the nineteenth, a romance was not a love story but a work of prose fiction that contained far-fetched, mysterious events. Romances of this period included English Gothic novels like *The Castle of Otranto* by Horace Walpole, a haunting story of ghosts and supernatural events, and the American author Nathaniel Hawthorne's *The House of Seven Gables*, an adventure of curses and mesmeric powers.

What exactly is a twentieth-century romance? Does it have any relationship with the lively, globe-trotting novels written today, with their fantastic plots of amorous intrigue? Or did the ever-cynical Oscar Wilde have it right in *The Picture of Dorian Gray*: "When one is in love, one always begins by deceiving oneself, and one always ends by deceiving others. That is what the world calls a romance."

Romances Through the Ages

THE VALENTINES	ORIGIN	SETTING
Leander and Hero	Mythological	Ancient Greece

Their fate: Leander drowns on his way to see his Hero, who upon hearing the news of his death flings herself into the sea.

Pyramus and Thisbe	Legendary/ mythological	Ancient Babylonia

Their fate: While Thisbe waits for Pyramus, she is frightened off by a lion, which smears blood on her dropped veil. A distraught Pyramus finds the veil by the mulberry tree where they were to meet. Thinking her dead, Pyramus kills himself. Thisbe does the same when she later finds Pyramus dead. Their blood supposedly turns to red the white fruit of the mulberry tree.

Narcissus and Echo	Mythological	Ancient Greece

Their fate: Echo pines for Narcissus, who does not return her love. She grows so weak that in the end only her voice remains, echoing her unrequited love. But, don't worry, Echo finally has her day: after Narcissus spurns her, she causes him to fall in love with his own reflection in a pool. He pines away *for himself*, then turns into the pretty narcissus flower. Question: why isn't there a flower called Echo?

Antony and Cleopatra	Real	First-century Egypt

Their fate: Antony commits suicide after hearing what is actually a false report of Cleopatra's death. It's believed that power-hungry, deceitful Cleopatra may have sent the report *herself*. Why? Because she wanted to please the ruler, Octavius, who hated Antony. Why? Because Antony abandoned Octavius's sister (whom he had married) for Cleopatra. Tune in next week. . . .

Abelard and Heloise	Real	Twelfth-century France

Their fate: Heloise, seventeen, falls in love with Abelard, a Catholic theologian, who is her tutor. After his career is ruined, she becomes a nun and he a monk. Seven centuries later, they are buried together.

Tristan and Isolde	Legendary	Medieval Ireland

Their fate: Sent to fetch Isolde as a bride for his uncle, Tristan falls desperately in love with Isolde (she reciprocates the feeling) after they drink a magic potion. The lovers separate; Tristan sends for Isolde on his deathbed, and she dies upon seeing him dead.

Romeo and Juliet	Fictional	Sixteenth-century Verona

Their fate: Because their families are sworn enemies, Romeo and Juliet marry secretly. The next day, Romeo stabs himself after finding what he thinks is Juliet's dead body. On waking from the sleeping potion, Juliet stabs herself over his lifeless body. The families announce they will *try* to get along.

91

....

| | | Nineteenth-century |
| Armand and Marguerite | Fictional | Paris |

Their fate: Accustomed to a life of luxury, beautiful Marguerite gives it all up for the penniless Armand. At Armand's father's urgent pleading, Marguerite reluctantly leaves Armand and returns to Paris. When Armand, then abroad, realizes her sacrifice, he rushes back to Marguerite, who dies in his arms. Greta Garbo starred as Marguerite in *Camille*, the film made from the novel *The Lady of the Camellias* by Alexandre Dumas, fils (son).

| | | Nineteenth-century |
| Gabriel and Evangeline | Fictional | Canada |

Their fate: Separated by political unrest in Nova Scotia, Evangeline and Gabriel spend years searching for one another. Evangeline, as an old woman, nurses a dying man whom she recognizes as her lover, Gabriel. She also dies and they are buried together. They are the main characters in the American poet Henry Wadsworth Longfellow's *Evangeline*, a long narrative poem.

| | | Nineteenth-century |
| Heathcliff and Cathy | Fictional | England |

Their fate: Childhood sweethearts, Heathcliff runs off to seek his fortune when he thinks Cathy no longer cares for him. Years after she marries a wealthy neighbor, Heathcliff returns to renew his love. Cathy resists and Heathcliff marries Cathy's sister-in-law for revenge. On her deathbed, Cathy admits that her heart always belonged to Heathcliff and to the wild, untamed moors. The novel, *Wuthering Heights* by Emily Brontë, was published in 1847.

What's in a Name?

Sometimes romance. Perhaps someone reading this book lives in a town in Louisiana called Eros. That's certainly a name with a romantic association, since Eros is the Greek god of love.

Look at a detailed state map. Can you find Lover, Pennsylvania; Love, Mississippi; Romance, Arkansas, or Kissimmee, Florida?

Do you see any other place names with ties to love?

The *Token* so *Charming*
changed my luck!
No longer *Melancholy*,
I'm *Moonstruck*!
We've set a *Date*
and planned our *Honeymoon*
with time to *Serenade*,
Croon,
Spoon, and *Swoon*.

Token

From the Old English word *tacen* comes *token*. The meaning of a keepsake, or a gift given as a sign of affection, can be traced back to Geoffrey Chaucer, writing in 1373: "Send hir letres tokens broches and rynges." It sounds like the poet might have been compiling a shopping list for Saint Valentine's Day: letter tokens, brooches, and rings!

Before 1653, all valentine tokens, cards, and gifts were hand delivered. In 1653, Paris set out the first mailboxes; reportedly, men who feared losing their jobs to the more convenient boxes put mice inside them to frighten away depositors.

When Oliver Cromwell seized power from England's King Charles I in 1653, he imposed strict moral standards. Under Cromwell's rule, exchanging valentine tokens was not tolerated. It was a low point for Cupid's followers. But after valentine Scrooge Cromwell fell from power in 1658, Valentine's Day celebrations were once again in full swing.

Early in the history of Saint Valentine's Day, it was the custom for both men and women to exchange tokens, in accord with names drawn in the love lottery. But by the seventeenth century, it was primarily the gentleman's responsibility to buy a gift.

Gloves and garters (and, of course, jewelry for those who could afford it) have proved the most popular valentine tokens, beginning in the early sixteenth century and continuing through the Victorian era. The following lines, written in the mid-seventeenth century, were typical of the times: "These garters, made of silken twine, / Were fancied by your Valentine."

Two hundred years later, some handsome valentine keepsakes were made by sailors away on long voyages. They carved and scratched designs into pieces of whalebone, walrus tusks, and shells, producing what is called "scrimshaw." Some of the scrimshaw pieces were designed to be used as corset stiffeners, or busks. One sailor carved these lines to his sweetheart on a corset busk made from a sperm-whale jaw.

> Accept dear girl, this busk from me
> Carved by my humble hand
> I took it from a sperm whale's jaw
> One thousand miles from land.
> In many a gale Had been the whale
> In which this bone did rest.
> His time is past, His bone at last
> Must now support thy breast.

During this period wood knitting sheaths and ivory or bone bobbins used in lacemaking were also carved with sentimental valentine messages, along with embroidered watch papers and brocaded hearts.

Perhaps one of the most delightful valentine tokens in the eighteenth century was a small volume of poetry. Some of these books were produced so that when the gilded pages were slightly fanned, a colored design spelled out the words, "To My Valentine."

The nineteenth-century valentine saved up his change to buy his sugarplum suitably inscribed porcelain boxes, jugs painted with an endless-knot-of-love motif, perfume bottles, and heart-shaped pieces of cotton or wool soaked with lavender scent.

Name me a swain today, devoted and true, who has the time or inclination to render his sweetheart's name in florid pen-and-ink swashes or have her name inscribed in a porcelain box.

Alas, eating out in restaurants and buying bouquets of flowers and pounds of fattening chocolate have, for the most part, eclipsed the more time-consuming and personal tokens of yesteryear.

 **Do You Know?**

Both garters and gloves, two popular valentine tokens, have interesting word histories. *Garter* comes from the Old Norman-French word *gartier*, which in turn is derived from the Old French *garet*, meaning "the bend in the knee," the very place where the garter came to be worn. Legend has it that in 1344, in England, King Edward III's dancing partner lost her garter. When the king picked it up, he did something surprising: he put it on his *own* leg. Anticipating raised eyebrows, King Edward said, "*Honi soit qui mal y pense,*" meaning "Shame on those who think ill of this." These French words later became the motto of the Order of the Garter, the highest order of knighthood in England.

The Old English word *glof*, or "palm of the hand," gives us *glove*. Ten-thousand-year-old gloves were discovered in northern Europe. Early peoples depended on these gloves, which were made of animal skins, to protect their hands from the cold and from the effects of hard work. Decorative gloves made of linen and tapestry were first worn by the Egyptians around 1500 B.C.

Charming

In fourteenth-century England, if you called your hostess a charming woman, the other guests would have fled the house. Six hundred years ago, someone who was charming was be-

lieved to be possessed by evil powers. In those days, charming people were not praised for their pleasant personalities!

Charm evolved from the Latin *carmen*, or "song." In Old French, a *charme* signified a chanting of a verse meant to evoke magical powers. "To charm the tongue" was a common phrase used in attempts to overcome these powers.

Later, *charm*'s meaning became more generalized and referred to objects thought to have supernatural force in warding off bad omens. Ornamental charms called "amulets" were often inscribed with symbols designed to protect the wearer from harm. Charm bracelets, worn since the 1860s, are the successors to these amulets and were worn decoratively because, by the sixteenth century, charm had taken on its more contemporary—and complimentary—meaning.

It was a logical transference of meaning from *charm* as an attractive personal ornament to *charm* as an attractive quality in one's personality. Yet, charm remains, in many ways, a mysterious quality and carries with it (as do the words *enchanting* and *bewitching*) some of the elusive magic of its original meaning.

Early valentines used charms as a way of winning a sweetheart. Three hundred years ago in England, it would not have been unusual for a young girl to sing a magic chant to stir up the spirit of a beau while running around the local church twelve times at midnight on the eve of Saint Valentine's Day.

Small children chanted on Saint Valentine's Day, hoping

to pocket a few pennies. As people threw coins from their windows, the parading children recited, "Tomorrow is come. Tomorrow is come."

Melancholy

The Greek words *melas*, "black," and *chole*, "bile," make up the word *melancholy*. In medieval times, people firmly believed that a person's physical and mental health were determined by the balance of four fluids in the body—blood, phlegm, black bile, and yellowish bile. These four fluids were called the "four humors."

If you had a ruddy complexion, you were supposedly governed by blood and were said to be brave, loving, and *sanguine*, which comes from the Latin word for blood, *sanguis*. Hot-tempered people were thought to have too much yellow bile, which accounted for their hostile outlook. Too much phlegm, on the other hand, reportedly caused sluggishness. From that we get our word *phlegmatic*, meaning slow-tempered and passive. Sad and thoughtful people reportedly suffered from an overabundance of black bile, which is secreted by the kidneys or spleen. They were said to be *melancholy*, which, as you know, means "black bile."

The next time someone accuses you of being down in the

101

dumps, just tell them it's probably because you have too much black bile in your system. You might also tell them that in sixteenth-century Rome, some of the most celebrated artists of all time were described as melancholic, among them Raphael and Michelangelo. In Queen Elizabeth I's court you would have gotten points for having a solemn air of melancholy about you. It was considered a mark of gentility and refinement. This attitude toward melancholy came to England from the French court.

Poets and writers never tire of writing about poetic pensiveness. Some, like those in Elizabethan England, looked upon it favorably, among them early seventeenth-century writer Robert Burton in his book *Anatomy of Melancholy*: "All my joys to this are folly, / Naught so sweet as melancholy." Nearly two hundred years later, the English poet John Keats continued to sing its praises in "Ode on Melancholy." "Ay, in the very temple of delight / Veiled Melancholy has her sovran shrine. . . ." Not everyone welcomed this sad, reflective state. As the poet William Cullen Bryant said in his poem *The Death of the Flowers*:

> The melancholy days are come, the saddest of the year,
> of wailing winds and naked woods, and meadows
>   brown and sere.

Apparently Oscar Wilde was right when he said, "Melancholy, that grave and beautiful word. How the poets love it."

Do You Know?

In the Middle Ages, if people referred to your "sense of humor" they were not discussing your funny bone. Those who practiced healing—and they weren't medical doctors—noticed that people who were ill discharged more fluids from their bodies than healthy people. This led the healers to encourage further fluid draining, such as bloodletting and purges, to release the "bad humor" they thought was responsible for keeping the body out of balance and causing the sickness. The problem was that these practitioners had no idea when to stop draining these fluids—as if draining did any good. They relied pretty much on their own "sense of humor" to determine the right proportion of fluids. Bloodletting was practiced into the late eighteenth century. At about the same time, humor also began to mean "mood" rather than fluid, and this is how we use the word today. Lulu, in a foul humor, returned Casanova's valentine brooch.

Moonstruck

People have always been awed and inspired by the moon. They have worshiped the moon—and even feared it. In this anonymous poem written about four hundred years ago, the author expresses concern for himself and his master.

Late late yestreen I saw the new moone,
Wi the auld moone in hir arme,
And I feir, I feir, my deir master,
That we will cum to harme.

Struck by the moon's beguiling powers, poets have scolded it for representing man's inconstancy. In William Shakespeare's immortale tale of star-crossed lovers, Juliet urges Romeo,

O, swear not by the moon, the inconstant moon,
That monthly changes in her circled orb,
Lest that thy love prove likewise variable.
(*Romeo and Juliet*, Act II, Scene 2, line 114).

Poets have also reserved some of their most beautiful language to describe the beauty of the moon: "That orbed maiden with white fire laden, / Whom mortals call the moon." (Percy Bysshe Shelley, "The Cloud").

Moonstruck comes from two Old English words, *mona*, "moon," and *strican*, "strike." From ancient times, people believed that the moon goddesses—the Greek goddess Selene and the Roman goddess Luna—could affect your mind. If you slept with your head exposed to moonlight, you were considered especially vulnerable to the moon's influence. Once "struck," people would begin to babble romantic nonsense, spend hours in a dreamlike stupor, or act mentally unbalanced. In 1846, Mrs. R. Lee made this entry in her African journal after sleeping in the open air on her travels: "I was afraid I was moonstruck." Apparently she wasn't, for she made no later reference to acting in a peculiar manner. No one is certain where this superstition originated, but it has been around for at least thousands of years; the ancient Egyptians also believed in the mysterious powers of the moon.

There are a number of other "moon" words that indicate the unsettling effects of the moon on mental states, among them *moonish*, *moonsick*, and *mooncalf*, which is a simpleton or a monster. Shakespeare's drunken butler, Stephano, prods the slave Caliban in these lines: "Moon-calf, speak once in thy life, if thou beest a good moon-calf." (*The Tempest*, Act III, Scene 2, line 24).

Lovers have also been accused of being moonstruck. In *David Copperfield*, Charles Dickens's favorite and most autobiographical novel, David writes, "I, the moon-struck slave of Dora, perambulated round and round the house and garden for two hours." Going around in circles also must have indicated a moonstruck condition.

Date

Our English word *date* comes from the Latin *data*, meaning "given." Letters sent from Rome began *data Romae*, or "given at Rome," followed by the day, month, and year.

Since the sixth century, people have set "dates," meaning a day and time indicated on a letter. But it wasn't until the nineteenth century that *date* was used to indicate a time and place for an appointment, and it wasn't until the twentieth century that *date* became associated with courting.

According to one story, it all began with young, unmarried men who worked on farms. Since these farmhands toiled long hours and had few days off, they had to set a date well in advance if they wanted to woo a young woman, who was often many miles away. This eventually led, it's thought, to calling the woman a date. Later, the noun led to the verb *to date*. Melissa took Brian as her date to the Halloween party. After dating for two years, they set their wedding date for February 14.

Honeymoon

Honeymoon comes from the joining together of two Old English words, *hunig*, "honey," and *mona*, "moon." The *moon* in *honeymoon* refers to the lunar month, or twenty-nine and a half days, and also to the fact that the full moon represents the happiest time for the couple, and as the moon wanes so, too, may their happiness. According to the English lexicographer Samuel Johnson, the author of *Dictionary of the English*

Language, published in 1755—unquestionably the most important linguistic work of the eighteenth century—*honeymoon* means "the first month after marriage, when there is nothing but tenderness and pleasure."

The *honey* part of *honeymoon* is not a slang reference to the bride but refers instead to the potent potion made of honey, water, malt, and yeast called "mead." Honeymooners consumed large quantities of mead during this one-month period to keep them on an even keel.

According to one historic report, the notorious barbarian king of the Huns, Attila, suffocated from drinking too much mead at his own wedding celebration.

Serenade

Crooning courtiers always hoped for a clear night for outdoor wooing. *Serenade* has its original nonmusical background in the Latin *serenus*, meaning "clear and fair," which was a reference to fair weather. When the word entered the Romance languages, it expanded from this base to mean "open air," as in Italian *sereno*. Later, Italian *serenata* meant a musical performance given in the open air. Eventually, in seventeenth-century England, the sense of fair and clear weather faded, and *serenade* became associated with a musical performance given at night, or specifically an evening song.

Richard Lovelace, a swashbuckling, handsome, aristocratic English poet of the first half of the seventeenth century, was noted for his graceful, fanciful love poems and songs. Lovelace was thrown into prison twice for supporting Charles I over Parliament (and its leader, foe to all valentines, Oliver Cromwell). It was in captivity that the poet wrote some of his most memorable lyrics, including this one from the poem, "To Althea, from Prison":

> Stone walls do not a prison make,
> Nor iron bars a cage;
> .   .   .   .
> If I have freedom in my love,
> And in my soul am free;
> Angels alone that soar above
> Enjoy such liberty.

Croon, Spoon, and Swoon

Here we have a wonderful trio of valentine words that rhyme. Say them in one breath and you're almost tempted to break into song. He crooned, handed her a spoon, she fell into a deep swoon.

Experts can find no trace of the word *croon* in Old English, though it does turn up in Middle English as *croynen*, which is derived from the Middle Dutch *kronen*, "to groan, murmur, or lament." In 1787, *croon* turned up in *The Holy Fair*, one of Robert Burns's long poems. He used it to describe a loud, deep sound, like that of a bell. "Now Clinkumbell, wi' rattlin tow, / Begins to jow an' croon." Translation: Now bellringer, with noisy bellrope, / Begins to ring and groan.

Later people likened the word *croon* to singing in a low, murmuring tone, particularly a popular song in a pleasing smooth voice. Bing Crosby was one of this century's most popular and famous crooners. And when he courted Rosemary Clooney in the movie *White Christmas*, you could say he was a spooning crooner.

Bing probably didn't bestow a set of valentine soup spoons on Rosemary, but early in English tradition, when spoons were the only eating utensils, courting sweethearts often exchanged spoons that were carved or engraved with the symbol of lovers' hands. This is almost certainly the origin of the verb *to spoon*, meaning to kiss and caress, though some people associate spoons with romance because the utensils customarily lie so close together in a drawer. The word *spoon* comes to us from the Old English word *spon*, which means a wood chip or shaving. In the fourteenth century, wood was first hollowed out to make eating utensils.

Swoon reaches us from the Middle English *swozene*, or *swuonen*, meaning "to fall into a fainting fit," which in turn is from the Old English *geswogen*, meaning "unconscious." In the sixteenth century, you might have overheard your overheated

armored neighbor complain, "Take my armour of / quickly, 'twill make him swoune, I feare." (Ben Jonson, *Every Man Out of His Humour*). People swooned when hot, when doing heavy labor, when distressed—"Home they brought her warrior dead; She nor swoon'd, nor utter'd cry." (Alfred Lord Tennyson, *Princess*)—or at the sight of something unpleasant: "Many will swoon when they do look on bloud." (William Shakespeare, *As You Like It*, Act IV, Scene 3, line 159).

During the nineteenth century, writers liked to incorporate *swoon* in their landscape descriptions. John Keats did it in his long allegorical poem *Endymion*, about a mythological Greek shepherd who begs for—and gets—eternal sleep so that he can dream forever of his love, the moon goddess Selene. "Strange ministrant of undescribed sounds, / That come a swooning over hollow grounds." Surely one of the most beautifully luscious swooning landscapes, inspired by a hot day in July, was that in Thomas Hardy's *Tess of the D'Urbervilles*: "Its heavy scents weighed upon them, and at mid-day the landscape seemed lying in a swoon."

Swooning fits were almost as common as sneezing in Victorian England. A bottle of vapors, or smelling salts, was always kept handy to aid a stricken lady in swooning distress. She may have been upset by bad news, bowled over by an especially extravagant or unexpected valentine token, or perhaps her corset was too tight. Or, could her swoon have been planned?

In one documented account, we know that a certain Victorian lady, who was expert at swooning on demand, was paid by a rather insecure pianist to attend a piano recital, during which he was scheduled to perform a demanding piece. The hired swooner represented a kind of insurance for the pianist. If he found he couldn't get through a tricky passage, he would make discreet eye contact with the woman, which was her cue to fall into one of her most convincing swoons. After she fainted, he would, as a concerned gentleman, stop the performance. So, he's off the hook, with his honor still intact. The hitch was that, during this one particular performance, either the swooner fell asleep or just lost attention. The pianist gave the signal, she didn't swoon, he fumbled a little more, then finally, in desperation, faked a seizure. And Liszt was spared. . . .

Do You Know?

A spoonerism actually has nothing to do with spoons. Named after the Reverend William A. Spooner of Oxford University, a spoonerism occurs when your tongue slips and you mistakenly switch the first letters of a group of words. William Spooner is famous for many such slips. For example, when he was marrying a couple, he leaned over and told the groom, "Son, it is kisstomary to cuss the bride."

Vappy Dalentine's Hay!

Timeline

This chart is meant to give readers a general time frame as well as specific points of reference to topics mentioned in this book.

....

2500	Chinese make ink from glue vapor and aromatic substances
995	David, second king of Israel, falls for Bathsheba, wife of one of his army captains
753	Legendary Roman ruler Romulus founds Rome
c.700	Numa Pompilius, second king of Rome, adds January and February to ten-month calendar
338	First Roman coins in existence
215	Construction begins on fourteen-hundred-mile-long Great Wall of China
0	Christian era begins
16	Diamonds are first mentioned in ancient writings
c.38	Mark Antony meets Cleopatra
c.100	Chinese make paper from plant fibers
107	Emperor Trajan sends ten thousand gladiators into the arena

249–260	Emperors Decius and Valerian try to destroy emerging Christian church
269	The priest Valentine is stoned and beheaded on February 14
305–311	Christian martyrs are killed by the thousands
313	Emperor Constantine the Great accepts Christianity
330	Constantine moves seat of empire to Byzantium, renamed Constantinople in his honor
407	Romans withdraw from Britain
450	Old English begins to develop in the British Isles
496	Pope Gelasius I turns pagan Roman festival of Lupercalia into a feast celebrating Saint Valentine
800	Charlemagne crowned Emperor of the West by Pope Leo III
802	First rose trees are planted in Europe
1066	Norman conquest of Britain begins; affects history, language, and literature
1100	Middle English period of the English language begins
1415	Charles, Duke of Orleans, sends rhymed valentines from the Tower of London
1526	Henry VIII meets Anne Boleyn and tries to divorce his wife
1536	Anne Boleyn is ordered executed by Henry VIII, her husband of three years—so much for true love

1594	Shakespeare writes *Romeo and Juliet*
1639	First Colonial post office set up in private Boston home—postmaster was paid one cent for every letter handled
1653	English puritanical leader Oliver Cromwell becomes Lord Protector of the Realm—bans Saint Valentine's Day customs
	First European post boxes appear in Paris, making sending valentines easier
1660	Stuart King Charles II is restored to English throne—Saint Valentine's Day celebrated again
1676	First poetry book by an American is published in Boston
1700	American colonists too busy with survival and colonization to fuss over Saint Valentine's Day
1740	Handmade valentines become popular in the colonies
1765	First chocolate mill erected in Dorchester, Massachusetts
1776	Frenchman invents lacemaking machine with seven hundred bobbin spools
c.1800	Valentine Writers, collections of romantic valentine verses, imported from England to America
1811	Young Swiss makes the first chocolate bar
1823	First rhyming dictionary published in New York City

1825	Tea roses introduced from China into Europe
	Sir Walter Scott, Scottish novelist, is identified as the anonymous author of the romantic Waverly novels
1830–50	Golden age of valentines in the United States
	Tom Thumb steam locomotive is first to pull passengers in England
1834	Robert Elton, a New York City engraver, produces first American valentine
1842	First adhesive postage stamp, a three-cent one, is issued February 15, in New York City
1844	Esther Howland receives a lacy valentine from England, and patents it in Worcester, Massachusetts
1847	Emily Brontë writes her poignant novel *Wuthering Heights*
1848	Alexandre Dumas, fils (son), writes a novel *The Lady of the Camellias*; nearly a century later Greta Garbo stars in the film *Camille*
1851	First Christmas card is designed and produced in Albany, New York
1857	Three million valentines sold in the United States, at three cents to thirty dollars apiece
1860	Esther Howland's valentine factory turns out thousands of valentines—sales reach $100,000
1863	On July 1, city mail delivery is in service in forty-nine cities, with 440 postal carriers

1880	Crude, cheap comic valentines are introduced, signaling an end to the age of romantic valentines
1884	Louis Waterman invents a fountain pen that works
1900	Thrifty valentines dine at self-service exchange buffet in New York City, where each dish costs one cent
1950	Thirty thousand rose varieties catalogued
	First couple selected by computer for marriage in Hollywood—where else?
1960	Pentel markets their first felt-tip Pentel pen
1989	Loveland, Colorado, post office reprocesses 300,000 valentines for remailing with its red postmark
1990	One dozen long-stemmed valentine roses cost as much as $100 on Saint Valentine's Day in major American cities

Bibliography

....

ETYMOLOGY

The Barnhart Dictionary of Etymology. New York: H. W. Wilson
   Company, 1988.
   Although smaller in scope than the more definitive *Oxford
   English Dictionary,* this very useful volume neatly weaves to-
   gether word derivations with historical facts.
The Oxford English Dictionary. Second edition. Oxford: Clarendon
   Press, 1989.
   This authoritative twenty-volume dictionary of word etymolo-
   gies not only provides historical record of how words have de-
   veloped and changed meaning but offers literary quotations that
   are as illuminating as they are fascinating.

LORE, MYTHOLOGY, AND INFORMATION

Brasch, R. *How Did It Begin?* New York: David McKay Company,
   1965.
   Traces roots and backgrounds of many familiar customs and tra-
   ditions. Creatively arranged, with index.
Funk, Wilfred. *Word Origins and Their Romantic Stories.* New
   York: Wilfred Funk, 1950.
   Folk etymology yarns spun by a pro.
Grun, Bernard. *The Timetables of History.* New York: Simon &
   Schuster, 1975.
   Encyclopedic in scope, this volume lists concurrent world events

117

in seven different fields of endeavor. Breadth and scope in a highly digestible presentation.

Kane, Joseph Nathan. *Famous First Facts*. New York: H. W. Wilson Company, 1981.
An exhaustive reference staple chock-full of some nine thousand first happenings.

Lee, Ruth Webb. *A History of Valentines*. New York: T. Y. Crowell Company (Studio Publications), 1952.
Sadly, out of print, but still the definitive book on valentine history, amply illustrated.

Mercatante, Anthony S. *The Facts on File Encyclopedia of World Mythology and Religion*. New York: Facts on File, 1988.

Panati, Charles. *Extraordinary Origins of Everyday Things*. New York: Harper & Row, 1987.
An entertaining and enlightening survey that points out the origins of over five hundred everyday items. The stories behind them are unfailingly fascinating.

Robertson, Patrick. *The Book of Firsts*. New York: Clarkson N. Potter, 1974.
A treasury of "firsts" information, well organized and indexed.

Senior, Michael. *The Illustrated Who's Who in Mythology*. New York: Macmillan, 1985.
A pictorial array of major gods and goddesses from world mythology.

Staff, Frank. *The Valentine and Its Origins*. New York: Praeger, 1969.
A valuable, well-illustrated supplement to Ruth Webb Lee's *A History of Valentines*.

Tuleja, Tad. *Curious Customs*. New York: Harmony Books, 1987.
A book that explores the sense—and nonsense—behind why we do what we do. A rich source of amusing sociological anecdotes.

Suggestions for Additional Reading

Barth, Edna. *Hearts, Cupids & Red Roses: The Story of the Valentine Symbols.* New York: Clarion Books, 1982.

Corwin, Judith H. *Valentine Fun.* New York: Messner, 1983.

Gibbons, Gail. *Valentine's Day.* New York: Holiday, 1986.

Guilfoile, Elizabeth. *Valentine's Day.* New York: Garrard, 1965.

Index

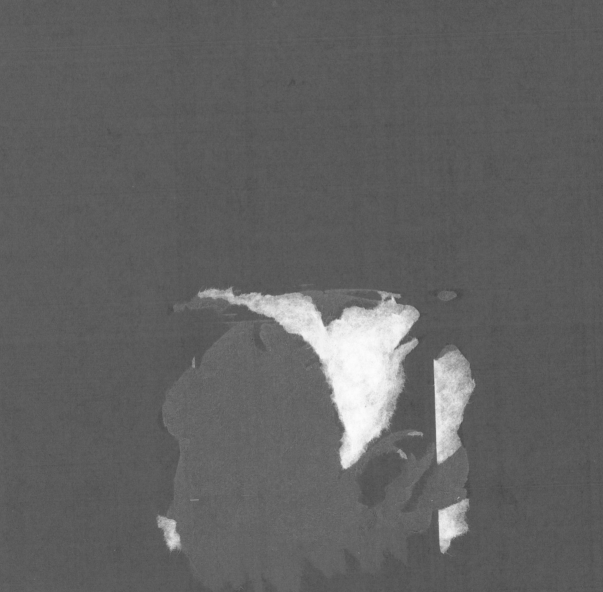